si ti ukuvela kwabantu si kuluma ngemva kwake, ngokuba a kw a-ziwa ukuma kwowokukqala. Si tsho ke ukuti sa vela nawo tina 'ba vele se ku tshiwo ukuti ama-tongo, ku tshiwo abapambili.

man: [illegible] men we speak of those who came after him, for the standing of the first man is unknown. So we, who came into being when men who preceded us already spoke of there being Amatongo, say, "We came into being possessed of them."

Kwa tsho abokukqala bonke ke; kwa ba aba velayo ba se be vela se be ba tshela wona amatongo, ba w' azi ke ukuti a kona amatongo. Kw azise futi ukuti kona kukqala ba ti be vela nje, ba be vela kanye nezinyanga ezona za ba kcansisela ukuti a kona. Ba ti ke, 'abiwa umuntu wokukqala, owa ti, "Ku kona amatongo a inyoka." Umu-ntu wokukqala Umvelinqangi, Unkulunkulu. 'Aziwa ke izizwe zonke. A kwa ba ko 'sizwe esa ti, "Tina 'basekutini ka li ko kwi-ti itongo."

All the first men, then, spoke of the Amatongo; and they told those who came into being after them, as soon as they came into being, that there are Amatongo. And further in the beginning, as soon as they came into being, they had doctors[3] who taught them that there are Amatongo. And so they said that the Amatongo were cre-ated[4] by the first man, who said, "There are Amatongo who are snakes." The first man is Umve-linqangi, Unkulunkulu. And thus all nations knew of the Ama-tongo. There was not a single nation which said, "We people of such a country have no Itongo."

Izizwe zonke za bonga amato-ngo, ngokuba kwa tsho Umveli-

All nations worshipped the Amatongo, because Umvelinqangi

[3] The izinyanga or doctors are thus represented as the appointed teachers of the people. They are, no doubt, the relic of an ancient priesthood.

[4] The native who relates this does not, he says, mean that when Unkulunkulu was speaking to primitive men, Amatongo were already in existence; but speaking of the future as already present, he appointed the spirits of the dead to be the protectors and helpers of the living:—that he said, "There are Amatongo," but the people looked around, but were unable to see them until death had deprived them of their parents, and then they addressed prayers to them, received visits from them in dreams, or in the form of snakes; and sacrificed to them.

n*q*angi, owa ba tshelako, wa ti, "Ni bona nje, into e ngi ni tshela yona; ngi ni tshela amatongo, ni bonge wona; ngi ni tshela izinyanga zokubula, ni bule kuzo, zi ni tshele uma umuntu e gula, e guliswa amatongo; zi ya 'ku li zwa ukuti u gula nje, u guliswa amatongo."

commanded them to do so, saying, "You see, then,[5] I tell you about the Amatongo, that you may worship them. I tell you about divining Izinyanga,[6] that you may enquire of them, and they tell you when a man has been made ill by the Amatongo; they shall hear the Itongo declaring that he has been made ill by the Amatongo."

Zonke ke izizwe ke za se zi ti, noma be ya 'ku*hl*asela empini; noko i ba bulala, ba ti, abakubo labo abafileyo be bulewe impi, ba ti, "Li si fulatele elakwiti itongo." Ba ti, "Ini ukuba abantu ba ze ba pele bonke, impi ku nga buyi noyedwa na, nomuntu na?"

So all nations used to think when they were about to attack an army, that they should be assisted by the Itongo; and although they were killed by the army, the friends of those who were killed said, "The Itongo of our people has turned its back on us." They asked, "How is it that all our people have at length come to an end, and not one man come back from the army?"

A ti um' e kona osindileyo, a ti, "Mina, ngi k*q*abuke, ngi sinda ke; ku be se ku tiwa nje, ma si pele sonke; kw ale umuntu wa ba munye; ngabe si te si k*q*edwa impi nje, yena owa be pi na? Ngi k*q*abuke, ngi sinda; ngi be ngi nga s' azi uma ngi za 'usinda, ngi bona abantu bonke bakwiti se be pelile."

If there is one who has escaped, he says, "As for me I escaped I know not how. The Amatongo had decreed that we should all die; one man[7] would not assent; when we were destroyed by the enemy, where was he I wonder? I escaped I know not how; I no longer expected to be saved, when I saw all our people destroyed."

---

[5] A mode of claiming attention, or commanding silence.

[6] *Izinyanga.*—It is, perhaps, better to retain the native word than to translate it by a word which does not fairly represent it. Inyanga, generally rendered *doctor*, means a man skilled in any particular matter = *magus*. Thus, an inyanga yokubula is a doctor or wise man of smiting, that is, with divining rods—a diviner. Inyanga yemiti, a doctor of medicines. Inyanga yensimbi, a smith, &c.

[7] That is, one man among the Amatongo—one of the Amatongo.

Ba ti ukukqala kwabo, ba ti, "Amadhlozi akwiti mabi! Ini ukuba umuzi u pelele empini wonke na? Amadoda angaka na! Impi ukupela na i kqedwe impi na! Kangaka a be fulatele, kw enze njani? Into a be nga i tsho si zwe uma kw' enza njani na? A ze a kqede umuzi na? u pele wonke na? Yena o kqabuke e sindisa ubani lo, u be ye ngapi na? U be nga hambi ini pakati kwamanye amadhlozi na?" Ba tsho njalo abakalayo.

At first the people say, "The Amatongo of our people are good for nothing! Why has the whole village perished in the fight? So many men as there were! Our whole army destroyed by the enemy! How did it happen that they turned the back on so many? How is it that they never mentioned any thing to us that we might understand why they were angry? Have they at last destroyed the whole village? has it come utterly to an end? Where had the Itongo who saved So-and-so gone? Why was he not among the other Amatongo?" Those who weep for the dead say thus.

Na labo abafayo empini se be ya 'kuba a wona amadhlozi futi.

And those who died in the fight will now become Amatongo.

Ba ti abasindileyo ab' amadhlozi akubo e ba bhekile, ba sinde, ba ti, "Si sindiswe amadhlozi akwiti." Ba fike ba buye, be vela empini, ba fike, ba wa gwazele izinkomo; ba bonge ukuba be ti a ba pilisile; ba zitele ngenyongo emzimbeni, be ti, "Ma kcakcambe, a be mhlope, a nga bi mnyama," ukuze a ba pilise ngolunye usuku futi. Ba bonge ku be kuhle.

And those who escaped, whose national Amatongo looked on them and saved them, say, "We have been saved by the Amadhlozi of our people." When they come back from the army, they sacrifice cattle to the Amatongo; they return thanks because they think they have saved them; they pour the gall of the sacrifices on their bodies, saying, "Let the Amatongo be bright and white, and not dark, that they may save us on another occasion." They return thanks with glad hearts.

Ku be ku kalwa ngalapa be file,

And there is funeral lamenta-

ku tiwe, id*h*lozi labo limnyama. Ba ze b' enzele ukuze ba ti noko nga inkosi yabo i ba pindelisa empini, i ti, ma ba *h*lasele, amad*h*lozi akubo a nga soli 'luto, ngokuba ba wa lungisile, ba wa kcakcambisa; se be ya 'kuti noko be fika kuyo impi se b' azi ukuti, "Umakazi loku sa wa lungisa amad*h*lozi, a ya 'kuti s' ona ngani na?" Lapa se be bona impi a ba ya 'kulwa nayo, ba kumbule amad*h*lozi, ba kcabang' izinto a ba z' enzayo, be wa kcola um' a be ma*h*le; ba ku bone loko en*h*liziyweni zabo, b' az' ukuti, sa wa lungisa amad*h*lozi akwiti; noko si fa, ka si yi 'kutsho ukuti i kona into a wa be e i kalela.

tion where they have lost their people; they say, their Idhlozi is dark. At length they sacrifice, that if perchance their chief lead them again to attack the enemy, the Amatongo of their people may have no cause of complaint, because they have made amends to them, and made them bright; and now when they reach the enemy they know what they have done, and say, "Can it be, since we have made amends to the Amadhlozi, that they will say we have wronged them by anything?" When they see the enemy with which they are about to fight, they remember the Amadhlozi, and think of what they have done for them, by sacrificing to them that they may be propitious; they see that in their hearts, and know that they have made amends to the Amadhlozi of their people, and that though they die they cannot say there is any thing of which the Amadhlozi have reason to complain.

Mbala ba tukutele ke, ba ti, "A ya 'kuba a si fulatele nje." Ngokuba uma be ya empini, ba ti, "Si hamba nawo amad*h*lozi akwiti," ba lwe ke nenye impi. A ti um' amad*h*lozi akubo em*h*lope, 'ale ukuba ba fe, ku be i bona be bulala abantu ngan*h*lanye, ba bone ke ukuti si be si hambe namad*h*lozi

So truly they are very brave, saying, "The Amatongo will turn their backs on us without cause." For when they go to the enemy they say, "The Amadhlozi of our people go with us;" and so they fight with the enemy. And if their Amadhlozi are white and do not allow them to die, and they kill on their side only, then they see that their Amadhlozi go with

akwiti. Ku ti kulabo abafileyo ba pike abaseleyo, ba ti, "A si namad*h*lozi. Ini uma si fe si pele na? Amad*h*lozi akwiti 'a*h*lulwe amad*h*lozi akwabanye abantu na?" Ngokuba be ti aba nga fanga, ba ti, "'A*h*luliwe amad*h*lozi akwabani, 'a*h*lulwe akwiti."

them. But on the part of those who are conquered, those who survive say, "We have no Amadhlozi. Why have we died utterly? Why have our Amadhlozi been conquered by the Amadhlozi of other people?" For those who have not died say, "The Amadhlozi of So-and-so have been conquered by the Amadhlozi of our tribe."

Ku njalo ke kubantu abamnyama; a ba velanga nje ukuba be ti, "Amatongo ka wa ko." Ba vela se ku tiwa, "Amatongo a kona." Kodwa ke nati ke ka s' azi uma lowo 'muntu owa vela kuk*q*ala wa za wa ti nje, "Ku kona amatongo." U kona ini umuntu owa ke wa ti e hamba wa be inyoka na? Ngokuba nati si ya ko*h*lwa lapo, uma Umvelin*q*angi wa za wa ti, id*h*lozi li inyoka nje, ngani. Loku umuntu e suka a fe nje e nge namsila; nati lapo ka si kolwa enyokeni; loku noma abantu be lele, u ti a nga pupa inyoka, a papame masinyane, 'etuke; a ti uma e pupa umuntu owa fayo, a kulume naye izindaba ekupupeni; inyoka umuntu e i pupa ka kalumi nayo izindaba, u y' etuka. Ngi ti mina, amad*h*lozi ka wa ko a nemisila. Umvelin*q*angi tina si ti w' eduka yena um' a t' abantu ba izinyoka. Ngokuba nabantu aba-

Thus it is with black men; they did not come into being when it was said, "There are no Amatongo." They came into being when it was already said, "There are Amatongo." But we do not know why the man which first came into being said, "There are Amatongo." Was there ever a man who whilst living said he was a snake? For we too do not understand why Umvelin*q*angi said, "The Idhlozi is a snake." For a man dies having no tail; and even we in that respect do not believe in a snake; for if a man is asleep, and dreams of a snake, he awakes immediately and starts; but if he dream of a dead man, he speaks with him of affairs in a dream; but if he dream of a snake, he does not talk with it; he starts. For my part, I say there are no Amadhlozi with tails. And we say Umvelin*q*angi made a mistake when he said, "People are snakes." For old men, when we ask why it

dala aba 'madoda si ti lapa si buzayo si ti, "Amadhlozi lawa ku tiwa a izinyoka nje ngani?" ba ti, "Ngoba kw amadhlozi." Si buze tina, si ti, "Ake ni si tshele abantu abafa be nemisila na?" Ba kohlwe lapa, ba nga si tsheli. Si ti ke, "O, ini ukuba ni nga si tsheli amadhlozi a izinyoka na?" Ba tsho njalo ke; ba kohlwa, ba nga si tsheli uma si zwe. Si y' ezwa uma be tsho amadhlozi enyokeni; ka si zwa uma inyoka i idhlozi.

is said that the Amadhlozi are snakes, say, "Because they are Amadhlozi." And we ask saying, "Just tell us if dead men have tails." They are puzzled there, and cannot tell us. And so we say, "O, how is it that you do not tell us whether the Amadhlozi are snakes?" So they repeat the same words; they are puzzled and do not tell us, that we may understand. We understand if they say, "The Amadhlozi are in snakes;" we do not understand if they say, "The snake is an Idhlozi."

Ukwaba equivalent to Create.

NJENGALOKO lapo inkosi ya tsho, ya ti, "A ku be kona ukukanya," kwa ba kona njengokutsho kwayo inkosi; si ti, "Kw' abiwa inkosi ukukanya." Ku njalo ke abantu ba ti, "'Abiwa amatongo Umvelingqangi." Ba ti futi, "Umuntu wokukqala w' aba amatongo, ukuti, wa wa veza." Ba ti, "Zonke izinto z' abiwa umuntu wokukqala, Unkulunkulu; z' enziwa uye;" ngokuba ku ya lingana ukwabiwa nokwenziwa.

JUST as when the Lord said, "Let there be light," and there was light in accordance with the word of the Lord; we say, "The light was created [abiwa] by the Lord." So the people say, "The Amatongo were created [abiwa] by Umvelinqangi." So they say, "The first man created [aba] the Amatongo, that is, he gave them being." They say, "All things were made by the first man, Unkulunkulu; they were made by him;" for ukwabiwa and ukwenziwa has one meaning.

Lapa tina ke, tina 'bantu si velayo, si ti, "Abantu abamnyama

We then, who come into being at the present time, now say,

ba lahleka. Ini ukuba ba ti ka ba m azi Umvelinqangi na? Abantu abaziyo abafundisi; bona be kuluma ngemiteto yenkosi. Yona si i zwayo igama layo, nendodana yayo. Si ya kohlwa uma yena umuntu wokukqala wa be ubani; loku si zwa Unkulunkulu Umvelinqangi; si ng' azi uba yena Unkulunkulu lo wa zalwa ubani.

"Black men are mistaken. Why do they say that they do not know Umvelinqangi? The people who know are the missionaries, who speak of the commandments of the Lord. We hear His name, and that of His Son. We do not know who the first man was; this only we hear, that Unkulunkulu is one with Umvelinqangi; not knowing who was the father of Unkulunkulu.

Loku abelungu ba fika nje nabafundisi, sa si li zwa igama lokuti, u kona Utikxo. Ku ya s' ahlula okutshiwo abantu, uma ku nga bi ko umuntu o ti Unkulunkulu wa dabuka kukqala nje, umfazi wake kwa ku ubani, nendodana yake. Loku indodana katikxo si ya i zwa ngabafundisi ukuti Ujesu. Si y' ahluleka; tina si ti ba lahleka. Ini uma ba si tshele Unkulunkulu? Si zwe ukuti be ti wa dabula izizwe zonke ezimnyama; si nga i zwa indawo lap' e kona a zi dabulela kona.

But since the white men came and the missionaries we have heard it said that there is God. We cannot understand what the black men say, for there is no one who tells us that Unkulunkulu first came into being, and what was his wife's name, and that he had a son. But we hear the missionaries say that Jesus is the son of God. We do not understand what the black men say. We say, "They are mistaken. Why do they tell us about Unkulunkulu? We hear them say that he created all the black nations; but we do not hear of the place where he created them."

Si kohlwe ke lapo kulabo 'bantu uma be ti s' enziwa Unkulunkulu, Umvelinqangi, (ukuti Umvelinqangi nje, ngokuba a vela kukqala

So we do not understand what these people mean, when they say we were made by Unkulunkulu, Umvelinqangi. He is called Umvelinqangi for no other reason but because he came into being first

ngapambili kwabantu.) Ba ti ke, "Wa memeza, wa ti, 'Ma ku vele abantu, ku vele izinto zonke, nezinja, nezinkomo, nezintete, nemiti, notshani.'" Kepa ke si ng' eze s' azi ezinhliziyweni zetu uma si zwa be tsho njalo, be ti izinto z' enziwe Unkulunkulu; si nga u zwa umfula owa be zi dabulela kona izizwe a z' aba Unkulunkulu.

immediately before men.[8] So they say, "He shouted saying, 'Let men come forth; let all things come forth,—both dogs and cattle, and grasshoppers, and trees and grass.'" But we could never understand in our hearts when we heard them say that all things were made by Unkulunkulu; and did not hear the name of the river where Unkulunkulu broke off the nations which he created [aba].

Si ti into e ize leyo kankulunkulu. B' eduka nobuula. A si i zwa into eyona y' enziwa Unkulunkulu. Tina si velayo si vela se be si tshela be ti s' enziwa Unkulunkulu. Si ti, "Into e ize. Ka i ko into yekqiniso lapo; ngoba a ba ko aba ti si y' azi lapa Unkulunkulu a dabulela kona abantu."

We say this matter about Unkulunkulu is a vain thing. They wandered with folly as a companion. We do not know a single thing that was created by Unkulunkulu. As soon as we were born they told us we were made by Unkulunkulu. We say, it is a vain thing. There is no truth in it; for there are none who say, they know the place where Unkulunkulu broke off the people.

Si ti tina si zwa abelungu,—zona izindaba zenkosi zi sezincwadini. Si ti, "Nampa abakuluma ikqiniso, be ti, 'Inkosi i kona.'" Na manje inkosi i kona. Nati si ti si vela kwa ku tiwa i kona inkosi; i sezulwini, ukuti Utikxo. Indaba

We say we understand the white men,—the true accounts of the Lord which are in books. We say, "Behold the men who speak the truth, when they say, 'The Lord is.'" And even now the Lord is. And we too say that from our birth it was said, the Lord is; He is in heaven; that is,

[8] Note again the force of *nga* before *pambili*: *pambili*, before—any indefinite time before; *ngapambili*, just before, immediately or a short time before.

kankulunkulu a si y azi; a i k*q*ondeki ka*h*le; insumansumane nje. Loku noma be ti, Unkulunkulu wa tuma unwaba, wa ti, a lu yokuti ezizweni zabantu, lu yokuti, abantu ma ba nga fi; ba ti, kwa ti ngasemva kwonwaba wa tuma intulwa ngasemva kwonwaba, unwaba se lu hambile ukuya 'kuti, abantu ma ba nga fi; ya hamba ngasemuva intulo ukuya 'kuti, ma ba fe. Kwa za kwa fika intulo kuk*q*ala; ya fika, ya ti intulo, abantu ma ba fe. Kanti unwaba lu libele ubukwebezane, ya za ya buya intulwa; kanti unwaba olu tunywa ukuk*q*ala, ka lu ka fiki, lu libele ubukwebezane. Lu te se lu ya 'kufika kubantu, se lu fika lu ti, "Ku tiwa, abantu ma ba nga fi." Ba se be ti abantu, k*q*ede lu memeze unwaba, lu tsho njalo, lu ti, "Abantu ma ba nga fi," b' ala abantu, ba ti, "Si bambe elentulo; se u kuluma ize wena; izwi e si li bambileyo, si bambe elentulo, yona i fike ya ti, 'Ku tiwa, Abantu ma ba fe.' Nant' igama e si li bambileyo. A si y azi leyo 'ndaba o i tshoyo, lunwaba." Tina ke si ti ke, mfundisi, si ti, izindaba zamanga; leyo 'ndaba i nge ko. Abantu b' enziwa inkosi. Unkulunkulu si ti wa kw azi ngani ukutuma izilwane ezihhuk*q*uzela ngesisu pansi, a ti i zona z' emuka za ya 'kukuluma kubantu indaba na? Si ti, ba ko*h*lwa.

God. We do not understand the account of Unkulunkulu; it is not easily understood; it is a mere fable. For although they say, Unkulunkulu sent a chameleon to go and tell the nations of men that men were not to die; and that after the chameleon he sent a lizard to tell men that they were to die; and the lizard arrived first and said that men must die. The chameleon forsooth loitered at a bush of ubukwebezane, until the lizard came back again, and the chameleon which was sent first had not yet arrived, stopping to eat the ubukwebezane. And when it came to men it said, "Unkulunkulu says that men are not to die." And when the chameleon had made this proclamation, men refused to listen, and said, "We have received the word of the lizard; what you now say is vain; the word which we have received is that of the lizard, which came and said, 'Unkulunkulu says, Man must die.' That is the word which we have accepted. We do not understand the matter, Chameleon, of which you speak." We thus say, Teacher, that these are false accounts; the tale is not real. Men were made by the Lord. We ask how could Unkulunkulu send animals which creep on their bellies, to take a message to man? We say they are deceived.

A si y azi indawo lapo Umvelinqangi abantu a ba vezela kona, uma ba be kona nje. I ya s' ahlula nati le 'ndaba; nabadala abafayo ba fa be nga l' azi lelo 'zwe lapa Unkulunkulu a dabulela kona abantu uma ba be kona; nabadala abasala kwabafayo ka ba tsho ukuti, si ya l' azi lelo 'zwe lapa Unkulunkulu a dabulela abantu; nabo ba ya dinga nje ukuba nabo b' ezwe ngendaba ukuti, Unkulunkulu wa dabula izizwe. A b' ezwakali abanye Onkulunkulu balezo 'zizwe a nga dabulanga Unkulunkulu wakubo. Tina se si ti uma si ba buza si ti, "Ake ni si tshele Unkulunkulu, si zwe," ba ti, "Ka s' azi." Si ti, "N' ezwa kanjani na ukuti kwa ku kona Unkulunkulu na?" Ba ti, "S' ezwa ngabantu abadala aba ngapambili kwetu." Si ti, "Labo aba be ngapambili kwenu b' ezwa ngobani na?" Ba ti ke lapo, "Si ya kohlwa; ka s' azi." Si ti, "Unkulunkulu wa be into e ize nje. Ini uma si ng' ezwa izindaba zake Unkulunkulu uku zi tshela zona izizwe a be z' enza Unkulunkulu na? Ku be i loku ni pika ngokuti kwa ku kona Unkulunkulu

We do not know the place where Umvelinqangi gave men being, that they might have life. Neither can we any more than our fathers understand this matter; and the ancients who are dead died without knowing the country where Unkulunkulu created men that they might have life; and the old people who are still living do not say they know the country where Unkulunkulu created men; and they too want to be told about the creation of the nations by Unkulunkulu. Other Onkulunkulu of those nations are not heard of, whom their own Unkulunkulu did not create.[9] And if we say to them, "Just tell us about Unkulunkulu, that we may understand," they reply, "We do not know." We say, "How did you hear that there was Unkulunkulu?" They reply, "We heard it of old men who were before us." We ask, "Of whom did those who were before you hear?" They say, "We cannot tell. We do not know." We say, "Unkulunkulu was a mere vanity. Why do you not understand the accounts of Unkulunkulu, which he told the nations which he made? Since you only assert continually that Unkulunkulu was, how can we understand

[9] He means that there is one supreme Unkulunkulu, from whom all other Onkulunkulu sprang.

njalo na? Si nga zi zwa izindaba zake na? Ka si kolwa."

UMPENGULA MBANDA.

what relates to him? We do not believe."

ABANTU ba ti ku kona amad*h*lozi abo. Ba ya kolwa kuloko, ngokuba ka b' azi ukuba umuntu u ya ngapi ekufeni kwake. Ba fumana ukuti ukupenduka inyoka ngokukcabanga kwabo. Ba ti umuntu u ya fa; ngemva kwaloku, uma e se file, a buye a penduke inyoka; ba ti ibizo lenyoka, ba ti, itongo; ba kuleka kulo ngoku li *h*labisa izinkomo, ngokuba ba ti izinkomo futi ezalo, ba zi piwa ilo; futi ba ti, ba pila ngalo; ku ngaloko be li *h*labisa izinkomo. Ba ti, uma be za 'ku li *h*labisa, ba buyise izinkomo en*h*le, uma be se z' alukile; noma zi se sekaya, ba zi butela 'ndawo nye noma zintatu noma zine; ka ba zi buti zonke; ba leta lezo ezi neyaku*h*latshiswa itongo, ba zi ngenise esibayeni; ba gakxe imvalo esangweni, be se be zi k*q*ok*q*ela. Umnikaziyo e se kuleka ematongweni, e ti, "Nansi inkomo yenu, nina 'bakwiti;" e se kuleka, e ba balisa oyise noninakulu a se

THE people say their Amadhlozi exist. They believe in that, for they do not know where men go when they die. When they thought of the matter they discovered that they turned into snakes. They say a man dies, and when he is dead, he turns into a snake; and they gave that snake the name of Itongo, and they worship it by sacrificing cattle, for they say the cattle too belong to it; it is it that gives them cattle; and they say it is by it they live; therefore they sacrifice cattle to it. When they are going to sacrifice, they bring home the cattle, if they have been driven out to pasture; or if they are still at home, they drive three or four together; they do not collect them all; they select those which are with the one they are about to sacrifice to the Itongo, and drive them into the pen; they close the gateway with poles, and then drive the cattle together in one place. The owner of the bullock having prayed to the Amatongo, saying, "There is your bullock, ye spirits of our people;" and as he prays naming grandfathers and grand-

ba fa, e ti, "Naku ukudhla kwenu; ngi ya kcela umzimba omnandi, ukuba ngi hambe kahle; nawe, banibani, u ngi pate kahle; nawe, banibani," e tsho njalo, e balisa ngabo bonke bakwabo a se ba fa. Emva kwaloko e be e se tata umkonto omunye o za 'ku i hlaba, e se nyonyoba, e se i gwaza emhlabankomo, ukuti eluhlangotini; i be se i kala, i ti, "Eh;" e be e se ti umniniyo, "Kala, nkomo yamadhlozi." E se pinda e balisa futi ngaloko, ngokuba e ti ba m nikela abakubo ukuba a hambe kahle ngaloko 'kukala kwenkomo. I be se i hlinzwa, se i pelile, umniniyo e be e se ka igazana elincinyane, e se sika umhlwehlwe futi, e se u tshisela ngasese negazana, e se li beke ngasese futi, e se tata impepo e se basa yona, e se beka umhlwehlwana pezu kwempepo, e ti, u pa abakubo usi olumnandi. Emva kwaloko ba be se be i dhla ke inyama. Ku pela.

mothers who are dead, saying, "There is your food; I pray for a healthy body, that I may live comfortably; and thou, So-and-so, treat me with mercy; and thou So-and-so," mentioning by name all of their family who are dead; and then the one who is going to kill the bullock takes an assagai and goes cautiously towards it, and stabs it in the place where the ox is usually stabbed, that is, in its side; and then the ox bellows, and the owner says, "Cry, ox of the Amadhlozi." And then he again mentions the Amatongo by name, because he thinks they have given him health, because of the cry of his ox. It is then skinned. When the skinning is completed, the owner takes a little blood, and cuts off a portion of the caul, and burns it in a secret place with the blood, which also he places in a secret place; and he takes incense and burns it, having placed the caul on the incense, thinking, he is giving the spirits of their people a sweet savour. After that they eat the flesh. That is the end.

Ku ti uma ku fe umuntu kubantu abamnyama a fulelwe ngamahlahla. Ku zinge ku hlolwa njalo umniniye lowo 'muntu ofileyo. Noma

When a man dies among black men the grave is covered over with branches. The person to whom the dead man belongs watches the grave continually. If

ku fe indodana uyise a linde njalo i*h*la*h*la, ukuze ku ti se be bona ukuba i*h*la*h*la li bunile ba dele, b' azi a ku ko 'luto olu nga m kipako, ngokuba u se bolile. Kepa uma e fumana inyoka ngapezulu, a tsho uma e se buyile lowo 'muntu o be yo*h*lola, a ti, "O, ngi m fumene nam*h*la nje e tamele ilanga ngapezulu kweliba."

a son has died, his father watches the branches constantly, that when they see that the branches are rotten they may be satisfied, knowing that nothing can now disturb the remains, for they are rotten. And if he observe a snake on the grave, the man who went to look at the grave says on his return, "O, I have seen him today basking in the sun on the top of the grave."

Ngaloko ke uma e nga buyi ukuya ekaya, be nga m pupi, ku *h*latshwe inkomo noma imbuzi, ku tiwe, u ya buyiswa en*h*le ukuba 'eze ekaya; ku ti uma be nga m pupi noma ku njalo, ba *h*lupeke ngokuti, "Lo 'muntu wa fa kanjani? a si m boni; itongo lake li mnyama." Ku yiwe enyangeni yobulawo uma ku umuntu womuzi

So then if the snake does not come home, or if they do not dream of the dead, they sacrifice an ox or a goat, and it is said he is brought back from the open country to his home. And if they do not dream of him, though the snake has come home, they are troubled and ask, "How did this man die? we do not see him; his Itongo is dark." They go to a doctor of ubulawo,[10] if it is the chief man

---

10 *Ubulawo*, A class of medicines, used for cleansing and brightening. Medicines used with the view of removing from the system something that causes dislike, and introducing into it something that will cause love.

There are two kinds used in each case—black ubulawo and white ubulawo; the black "washes," the white "wipes;" the black takes away the "blackness"—"the evil,"—which causes a man to be disliked; the white makes him "white"—causes him to be "bright"—gives him a "beauty,"—which causes him to become an object of love and admiration.

Both black and white ubulawo are roots of plants.

The black is first used. The roots are bruised, mixed with water, and "churned:" when a great deal of froth has been produced by the churning process, it is drunk and the body is washed with it. It is used for about a month. The first time of using it, the medicines are taken to some place where the aloe is abundant; there a large fire is kindled of aloe; and the medicine being prepared is drunk in large quantities; it is emetic, and the contents of the stomach are ejected

omkulu; ai, a ku tshiwo ngabantu kazana nje. Inyanga i fike i pe*h*le ubulawo, ku *h*latshwe imbuzi, yona i nomsindo nokukala; imvu a i *h*latshwa ngokuba ku tiwa itongo li ya 'kuba mnyama, ngokuba imvu i isiula, a i namsindo; a ku vamile ukuba ku *h*latshiswe itongo ngemvu; itongo li *h*latshiswa ngembuzi, yona ku ti umuntu e sa i ti k*c*hu ngosungulo, i be se i bangalasa, ba tokoze ke kakulu, ba ti, "Kala, nkomo kabani, owa ti, wa ti, wa ti" (be tsho izenzo zake). Ba ti, "Si ti, Buya u ze 'kaya, si ku bone nam*h*la nje. Si ya *h*lu-

of a large village; but nothing is done as to the poor. The doctor comes and mixes ubulawo, and a goat is killed, it being an animal which makes a great noise and cries; but a sheep is not killed, because it is said it will cause the Itongo to be dark; for a sheep is foolish and makes no noise, and therefore it is not usual to sacrifice a sheep to the Itongo. The Itongo has a goat sacrificed to it; when a man pricks it with a needle, it at once makes a great noise; and so they rejoice greatly and say, "Cry, beast of So-and-so, who did such and such and such things" (mentioning the things he did). "We say, Come home again, that we may now see you. We are trou-

---

into the fire so as to quench it; the object being that the "badness," which is cast off, may be burnt up and utterly consumed. On subsequent occasions the contents of the stomach are ejected on pathways, that others may walk over it, and take away the "insila" or filth that is the cause of offence which has been cast out.

When the treatment by the black ubulawo has been continued for the proper period, the white is used much in the same way. The roots are bruised, mixed with water, and churned. If the man is using it because he has been rejected by some damsel, he adds to the medicine something belonging to her which has been worn next her skin, especially beads; whilst churning the medicines he praises the Amatongo, and prays for success. When the froth is produced and rises high above the mouth of the pot, he allows it to subside; and then takes some of the froth and puts it on his head and sprinkles it over his body; and then drinks the contents of the pot. It has an emetic effect. But the contents of the stomach are ejected in the cattle-pen. This place is selected because the white ubulawo is a "blessing."

The special circumstances under which such medicines are used are when a youth has been rejected; or when a man wishes to obtain a favour from a chief or great man; or when he has been summoned by the chief to answer a charge brought against him; or under the circumstances narrated in the text. But in the case of "bringing home" the Itongo, the white ubulawo only is used.

peka, uma si nge se sa ku bona, si ti, u si sola ngani na? loku izinkomo ezako zi mi nje; uma u biza inyama, u nga tsho zi *h*latshwe, ku ng' ali 'muntu."

bled if we never see you, and ask, why you are angry with us? for all the cattle are still yours; if you wish for meat, you can say so, and the cattle be slaughtered, without any one denying you."

Y elape ke inyanga leyo yobulawo, i bu pe*h*le i m biza, bu bekwe emsamo. I tsho ukuti, "Ngi ti u za 'ku m bona nam*h*la nje, u kulume naye; noma kade u nga m boni, nam*h*la nje u ya 'u*h*lambuluka.

So the doctor of ubulawo practises his art; he mixes the ubulawo, calling the dead man by name, and puts the ubulawo in the upper part of the hut, and says, "I say, you will see him to-day, and talk with him; although you have not seen him for a long time, to-day he will be clear."

Ku njalo ke ukuyiswa kwesituta, si buyiswa ngenkomo na ngobulawo.

Such then is the means employed to bring back a ghost; it is brought back by sacrifice and ubulawo.

The people do not worship all Amatongo indifferently.

ABANTU abamnyama a ba kuleki ematongweni onke, abantu abafayo bakubo; kakulu ku kulekwa en*h*lokweni yalowo 'muzi kulabo 'bantwana balowo 'muzi; ngokuba abadala abafako a ba b' azi nezibongo zabo uma kwa ko obani na. Kepa uyise a ba m aziko u in*h*loko yokuba ba k*q*ale ngaye, ba gcine ngaye ekukulekeni, ngokuba ba ya m azi yena kakulu, na ngoku ba tanda kwake abantwana bake; ba ya kumbula uku ba pata kwake e se kona, ba linganise loko 'ku ba

BLACK people do not worship all Amatongo indifferently, that is, all the dead of their tribe. Speaking generally, the head of each house is worshipped by the children of that house; for they do not know the ancients who are dead, nor their laud-giving names, nor their names. But their father whom they knew is the head by whom they begin and end in their prayer, for they know him best, and his love for his children; they remember his kindness to them whilst he was living; they compare his

pata kwake e se kona, ba ku mise nokuti, "U sa 'ku si pata kanjalo noma e file. A s' azi uma u ya 'kubuye a bheke aobani ngapandhle kwetu na; 'kupela u ya 'kubheka tina."

Ku njalo ke noma be kuleka kwamaningi amatongo akubo, b' enza ugange olukulu lwoku ba vikela; kepa uyise u dhlulisisile ekupatweni kwamatongo amanye. Uyise u igugu kakulu kubantwana bake noma e nga se ko. Ku ti labo a se be kulile be m azisisa kakulu ukuba-mnene kwake nobukqawe bake. Ku ti uma ku kona ubuhlungu pakati kwomuzi, indodana enkulu i m bonge ngezibongo zake a zi zuza umhla e lwa empini, a wa weze ngamazibukwana onke; i m tetisa ngokuti, "Ku nga ze ku fe tina nje. U se u bheke 'bani? A si fe si pele, si bone uma u ya 'ungena pi na? U ya 'kudhla izintete; ku sa yi 'kubizwa 'ndawo uma u bulale owako umuzi."

treatment of them whilst he was living, support themselves by it, and say, "He will still treat us in the same way now he is dead. We do not know why he should regard others besides us; he will regard us only."

So it is then although they worship the many Amatongo of their tribe, making a great fence around them for their protection; yet their father is far before all others when they worship the Amatongo. Their father is a great treasure to them even when he is dead. And those of his children who are already grown up know him thoroughly, his gentleness, and his bravery. And if there is illness in the village, the eldest son lauds him with the laud-giving names which he gained when fighting with the enemy, and at the same time lauds all the other Amatongo; the son reproves the father, saying, "We for our parts may just die. Who are you looking after? Let us die all of us, that we may see into whose house you will enter.[11] You will eat grasshoppers; you will no longer be invited to go any where, if you destroy your own village."

[11] That is, they suggest to the Itongo, by whose ill-will or want of care they are afflicted, that if they should all die in consequence, and thus his worshippers come to an end, he would have none to worship him; and therefore for his own sake, as well as for theirs, he had better preserve his people, that there may be a village for him to enter, and meat of the sacrifices for him to eat.

Ngemva kwaloko ke ngoku m bonga kwabo, b' em' isibindi ngokuti, "U zwile; u za 'kwelapa, izifo zi pume."

After that, because they have worshipped him, they take courage saying, "He has heard; he will come and treat our diseases, and they will cease."

Ku njalo ke ukutemba kwabantwana etongweni eli uyise.

Such, then, is the faith which children have in the Itongo which is their father.

Futi uma ku kona inkosikazi yomuzi eyona i zala abantu, noma indoda i nga file, itongo layo li ya patwa kakulu indoda yayo nabantwana bonke. Leyo 'nkosikazi i itongo lokubonisa umuzi. Kepa kakulu uyise njalo o yena e in*h*loko yomuzi.

UMPENGULA MBANDA.

And if there is a chief wife of a village, who has given birth to children, and if her husband is not dead, her Itongo is much reverenced by her husband and all the children. And that chief wife becomes an Itongo which takes great care of the village. But it is the father especially that is the head of the village.

KU tiwa ku kona itongo, inyoka. Ba pupe. Ba ti, ba nga pupa, a be se u ya gula; a ti, "Ngi gula nje, ngi pupile." Ba buze abanye, ba ti, "U pupe ni na?" A ti, "Ngi pupe umuntu." Uma kwa buba umfo wabo, a ti, "Ngi bone umfo wetu." Ba buze, ba ti, "U be e ti ni na?" A ti, "Ngi m pupe e ngi tshaya, e ti, 'Kwa be u sa ng' azi na ukuti ngi kona na?'" A ti, "Ngi m pendulile, nga ti, 'Uma ngi ya kw azi, nga u bona, ng' enze njani na? Ngi ya kw a-

IT is said that there is the Itongo,[12] which is a snake. Men dream. A man dreams perhaps, and is then ill; he says, "I am ill for no other reason than because I have dreamed." Others ask him what he has dreamed. He tells them he has dreamed of a man. If his brother has died, he says, "I have seen my brother." They ask what he said. He says, "I dreamed that he was beating me, and saying, 'How is it that you do no longer know that I am?' I answered him, saying, 'When I do know you, what can I do that you may see I know you? I know that you

[12] The *Itongo*,—a collective term meaning the inhabitants of the spirit-world, or abapansi.

zi, uma umfo wetu.' Wa ngi pendula, kqede ngi taho njalo, wa ti, 'U ti uma u hlaba inkomo, u nga ngi pati ini na?' Nga ti, 'Ngi ya ku pata, ngi ku bonge ngezibongo zako.' Nga ti, 'Ake u ngi tshele inkomo e ngi i hlaba, a nga ku pata. Loku nga i hlaba inkabi, nga ku pata; nga i hlaba inyumbakazi, nga ku pata.' Wa pendula, wa ti, 'Ngi ya i tanda inyama.' Nga m pikisa, nga ti, 'Kqa, mfo wetu, a ngi nankomo; u ya si bona ini esibayeni na?' Wa ti, 'Neyodwa, ngi ya i biza.' U ti, nga ba se ngi ya papama, kwa se kubuhlungu esikaleni; nga ngi yati ma ngi pefumule, kw' ala; kwa nqamuka umoya; nga ngi yati ma ngi kulume, kw' ala; kwa nqamuka umoya."

Wa kqinisela, ka vuma uku i hlaba inkomo. Wa gula kakulu. Wa ti, "Kona ngi gula nje, ngi ya si bona isifo esi ngi gulisayo." Ba ti abantu, "U si bona njalo, ku si lungisi na? Umuntu a ng' enza ngamabomu isifo esi mu gulisayo; e si bona, a tande ukuze a fe na? Lok' umhlaba, uma se u tukutelele umuntu, u ya mu tshonisa na?"

are my brother.' He answered me as soon as I said this, and asked, 'When you sacrifice a bullock, why do you not call upon me?' I replied, 'I do call on you, and laud you by your laud-giving names. Just tell me the bullock which I have killed without calling on you. For I killed an ox, I called on you; I killed a barren cow, I called on you.' He answered, saying, 'I wish for meat.' I refused him, saying, 'No, my brother, I have no bullock; do you see any in the cattle-pen?' He replied, 'Though there be but one, I demand it.' When I awoke I had a pain in my side; when I tried to breathe, I could not; my breath was short; when I tried to speak, I could not; my breath was short."

The man[13] was obstinate, and would not agree to kill a bullock. He was very ill. He said, "I am really ill, and I know the disease with which I am affected." The people said, "If you know it, why do you not get rid of it? Can a man purposely cause the disease which affects him; when he knows what it is, does he wish to die? For when the Itongo[14] is angry with a man, it destroys him."

---

[13] The narrator from this point appears to relate something he has actually known, and not any hypothetical case.

[14] *Umhlaba*, the earth, is a name given to the Amatongo, that is,

A ti, "Amanga, madoda; ngi njenje; ng' enziwa umuntu. Ngi ya m bona ebutongweni, ngi lele; u ti, ngokuba u tanda inyama, u ngi kwele ngamakcebo; u ti, ngi be ngi sa *h*laba inkomo, ngi nga mu pati. Ngi ya mangala ke mina, loku izinkomo ngi zi *h*laba kangaka; a ku ko inkomo e nga i *h*laba, a nga za nga m pata; zonke izinkomo e ngi zi *h*labayo, ngi ya mu pata; noma ngi *h*laba imbuzi, ngi ya m pata; ngi be ngi ya *h*laba imvu, ngi m pate. Ngi ti kodwa mina, u y' ona; a nga ti, uma e zibizela inyama, a ngi tshele nje, a ti, 'Mfo wetu, ngi tanda inyama.' A ti kumina, a ngi ze ngi nga m bonga. Mina ngi tukutele, ngi ti, u tanda uku ngi bulala nje."

He replied, "Not so, Sirs; I am thus ill; I have been made ill by a man. I see him in sleep, when I am lying down; because he wishes for meat, he has acted towards me with tricks, and says that when I kill cattle, I do not call on him. So I am much surprised for my part, for I have killed so many cattle, and there is not one that I killed without calling on him; I always called on him when I killed a bullock. And if I kill a goat, I call on him. And whenever I kill a sheep, I call on him. But I say, he is guilty of an offence; if he wished for meat, he might just tell me, saying, 'My brother, I wish for meat.' But he says to me that I never laud him. I am angry, and say he just wants to kill me."

---

the Abapansi, or Subterraneans. We find such expressions as these:—"U guliswa um*h*laba," The Itongo has made him ill. "U bizwa um*h*laba," He is summoned by the Itongo,—that is, he will die. "U petwe um*h*laba," He has been seized by the Itongo. "U tshaywe um*h*laba," He has been smitten by the Itongo. "U nom*h*laba,"—"U netongo," An Itongo has entered into him and is causing disease.

Umhlaba is said to be an *ukuhlonipa* word. The following words are also applied to the Ancestral Spirit:—Itongo, Id*h*lozi, Isituta. We also have Izinkomo zomzimu. Among the Amazulu, Umzimu is a word used only in this connection, and appears to be a collective term for the Amatongo. But on the Zambesi, Azimo or Bazimo is used for the good spirits of the departed. (*The Zambesi and its Tributaries. Livingstone, p. 520.*) Compare also Note above, p. 93. There is also another word, Unyanya, which is used in the same way as Itongo. Thus a man who has been fortunate says, "Ngi bhekwe Unyanya," I have been regarded by Unyanya. Among the Amalala, we meet with another word, Und*h*lalane, pl. Ond*h*lalane. Thus they say, "Und*h*lalane u ngi bhekile," Und*h*lalane has regarded me, that is, the Itongo. "Ond*h*lalane ba ngi bhekile," The Ond*h*lalane have regarded me.—These words are probably the names of some great ancestors, who, though now forgotten, were formerly especially remembered and worshipped for their great and good deeds whilst living.

Ba ti abantu aba m bonayo lapa e gulayo, ba ti, "Au! Lo 'muntu, u ti, u sa ku kqonda ini ukukuluma na? Si kuluma nawe nje ke; u pi na, kona nati ngapana si m buza na? Loku nati ku se u hlaba izinkomo; lapa u bonga, si kona u bonge, u m bonge, u m pate ngezibongo zake zobukqawe; nati si zwe. U ti, uma ku be, wena kabani na, uma ku be umfo wenu lona na, noma umuntu u fa kqede, a buye a vuke, nga si nga m buzi na, ukuti, 'U tsho ngani na?—loku Ubani u hleze e hlaba izinkomo izikati zonke, ku se e ku bonga, a ku bonge ngezibongo zako zobudoda; nati si zwe.'"

The people who see him when he is ill say, "Au! Do you mean to say that the man[15] still understands how to speak? We speak with you now; where is he, that we too might take him to task? For we too were present at all times when you slaughtered cattle; and when you lauded, you lauded him, and called upon him by the laud-giving names which he received for his bravery; and we heard. And, Son of So-and-so, if it could really be that that brother of yours, or any other man who is already dead, should rise again, could we not take him to task, and ask, 'Why do you say so?—since So-and-so is continually killing cattle, and lauds you with the laud-giving names which you received for your manliness; and we too heard.'"

A ti "Ehe!" o gulayo; "a ti u gabe ngokuba e ti umfo wetu omkulu; ngokuba mina ngi muncinyane. Ngi ya mangala uma u ti, ma ngi kqede izinkomo nje. Yena wa fa e nge nazo ini na?"

The sick man replies, "Eh! My brother acts in this boastful way because he says he is oldest; for I am younger than he. I wonder when he tells me just to destroy all the cattle. Did he die and leave none behind?"[16]

Ba ti, "Au, umuntu wa fa, wena kabani. Tina si ti, uma si kuluma nawe nje, amehlo ako e sa

They say, "Au, the man died, Son of So-and-so. For our parts we say, when we are really speaking with you, and your eyes are

[15] That is, he who is dead.

[16] "Did he die and leave no cattle behind?"—Since he did not sacrifice all his cattle to the Amatongo, but left some when he died, why should he be so unreasonable now he is an Itongo as to demand that I should sacrifice all mine?

bhekile nje,—tina si ti, lo 'muntu u nga u kuluma nje; noma u nembuzi, u m bonge. Kodwa si ti, u nehlazo um' a be se u ya ku bulala, a nga ku tsheli kahle, nawe u kqonde; u be u sa nga m pupa izikati zonke, u be se u za 'kugula na. Ipupo libi. Ini umfo wenu u b' u sa nga m bona u lele, u be se u ya gula na? Ku nani umuntu e pupe umfo wabo, a vuke umzimba umnandi, a tshele abantu a ba lauzele ukuti, 'Umzimba wami u polile, umnandi.' A ti, 'Ngi pup' umfo wetu e kuluma izindaba ezinhle kumina.' A ti, a nga fika izikati zonke kuwe, u fika ngempi, se u ya gula; se s' azi ukuti u gula nje ke, u ya 'kuba u pupe umfo wenu nje."

still really looking upon us,—we say, as regards that man, you should just speak quietly with him; and if you have a goat only, worship him with it. But we say it is a shame in him to come and kill you, without telling you properly, that you may understand. But you are dreaming of him constantly, and are then ill. It is a bad dream. Why do you constantly see your brother in your sleep, and become ill? It were well that a man should dream of his brother, and awake with his body in health, and tell the people his dream, saying, 'My body is now restored to health; it is without pain. I have dreamed of my brother, telling me pleasant news.' But now he comes to you at all times with hostile intent, and you are ill; and so we know that you are ill on that account, because you dream of your brother."

A ti, "Ehe, madoda, mina se ngi za 'ku mu nika inyama yake a i tandako; lokw e ti kumina ngi nga m pupa; u ya i pata inyama; u ya ngi bulala; ngi ti, ku nani uma a fike kumina ebusuku, ngi lele, a ngi tshele kahle, a ti, 'Mfo wetu, ngi tanda ukuti,' si kulume naye kahle, ku bonakale ukuti ngi pupe umfo wetu? U y' ona, ku

He says, "Eh, Sirs, I will now give him the flesh he loves; for he speaks to me when I dream of him; he demands flesh; he kills me; I say, what prevents him from coming to me by night when I am asleep, and telling me quietly, saying, 'My brother, I wish so-and-so,' that we may talk pleasantly with each other, and it be evident that I have dreamed of my brother? He wrongs me; daily I

ya sa ngi ya m pupa, ngi vuke ngi nenzeba; ngi ti, ka 'muntu; into e ya be ishinga, i tanda ukulwa nabantu. Kodwa, madoda, si be si da si zwa ni ti, 'Umuntu owa fa e ishinga eli nga kulumiswayo abantu, id*h*lozi lake li be li*h*le na?' Si be si da si zwa ni tsho njalo, ni ti u t' a nga fa, itongo lake li lunge, li be li*h*le. Kanti ku lunga umuntu owa be lunge kade. Um*h*laumbe a ti nowa be lungile, a fike a be mubi uma e file; nowa be ishinga, a ti uma 'se file, a lunge, a be umuntu o 'tongo li*h*le. Ku ya fana loko kokobili. Si ya ni pikisa nina, nina ni ti umuntu owa fa e ishinga e nga kulunyiswa, a ti a nga fa, a be ned*h*lozi eli*h*le. Tina si ti ku ya fana nje; nowa be lungile, u ya vuka a be u*h*lanya lapa 'se file; ka ku muki ngokulunga kwake um' e sa hamba ngapezulu; no*h*lanya lu fa k*q*ede, lu lunge, lu be id*h*lozi eli*h*le."

dream of him, and then awake in suffering; I say, he is not a man; he was a thing which was a wretch, which liked to fight with people. But, Sirs, we have been accustomed to hear you say, 'As to a man who died being a wretch, one of a word and a blow, is the Idhlozi of such an one good?' We have been accustomed to hear you say thus, that when he is dead his Itongo becomes right and is good. But forsooth that man is good who had been good long before his death. Perhaps he too who was good becomes bad when he is dead; and he who was bad, when he is dead, is good, and becomes a good Itongo. Both are alike. We deny the truth of what you say, when you assert that a man who died being a wretch of a word and a blow, when he is dead, may have a good spirit. We maintain that the two things are alike; both he who was good will be a wrathful man when he is dead; it does not turn out in accordance with his righteousness which he had when he was still living on the earth: and the wretch when he is dead becomes righteous and becomes a good spirit."

Ba ti, "Ehe, si ya ku vumela; u k*q*inisile. Ku ya fana kokobili."

They say, "Ehe, we agree with you; you speak the truth. The two things are alike."

A ti, "Ngi ti ke, umfo wetu u

He replies, "I say then, my

muke nobushinga bake uma e sa hamba ngapezulu kwom*h*laba; noma e se file, id*h*lozi lake li fana naye e sa hamba ngapezulu, ngokuba yena u be nga kulumiswa. U be ti umuntu a nga kuluma naye, a tande ukuba a be se u ya lwa naye. Ku be ku nga fika ikcala; l' enziwe uye, a be se u ya lwa, a nga ku boni ukuti, 'Konje nje leli 'kcala l' enziwe umina; a ku fanele ukuba ngi lwe nabo laba 'bantu;' esuke a tande yena uku ba bulala abantu. Ned*h*lozi lake li njalo; libi; li ya tukutela; u ti uma 'se tukutele a lete izilwane. Kodwa mina ngi ya 'ku mu nika inyama yake a i funa kumina. Ngi lele ebutongweni, ngi ya vuka, e se ngi nike isifo emzimbeni wami. Ngi za 'ku mu nika. Uma ngi bone ke, ma ngi yeke, ngi pile, ngi ya 'ku zi *h*laba izinkomo kusasa; uma e nga ngi yekile, ngi ya 'ku zi yeka, ngi ya 'kuti, 'Ka si yena umfo wetu.' Uma ku uyena, ma ngi pile, ngi pefumule, ku yeke ukun*q*amuka umoya, njengaloku ngi n*q*amuka umoya nje."

brother has gone away with his wickedness which he exhibited whilst living on the earth; and though he is dead, his spirit resembles him whilst he was alive, for he was a man of a word and a blow. If a man spoke to him, he used to wish at once to fight with him; and then a dispute might arise; it was caused by him, and then he would fight, and did not see it nor say, 'So then the fault was committed by me; I ought not to fight with these people;' but he started up and wished to injure the people. And his spirit is like him; it is wicked; it is constantly angry; and when it is angry it sends animals.[17] But I will give him his flesh which he demands of me. I sleep, and when I awake find that he has affected my body with disease. I will give him; if I see that he leaves me and I am well, I will kill some cattle in the morning; if he does not leave me, I will have the cattle, and say, 'It is not my brother.' If it is he, let me get well and breathe, and my breath no longer cut me, as it cuts me at the present time."

---

[17] *A lete isilwane.*—Ukuleta isilwane, ngesinye isikati amatongo a zibonakalisa ngemi*h*lola, ku ngene isilwane; amagama ezilwane ku kona isalukazana nentulwa; nge-

They bring Animals.—As regards bringing animals, sometimes the Amatongo manifest themselves by signs, and animals enter the village; the names of the animals are isalukazana and other lizards;

Ba vuma ba ti, "Ehe, wena kabani na; ma ku se kusasa se u sindile, s' and' uma si bone uma ilona id*h*lozi lomfo wenu; uma ku sa u sa gula, a si yi 'kutsho ukuti

They assent and say, "Yes, yes, Son of So-and so; if in the morning you are well, then we shall see that it is indeed the spirit of your brother; if in the morning you are still ill, we will not say it is

---

sinye isikati inyoka e nge si lo itongo; kumbe ku fike inyamazane ekaya; ku tatwe izibulo, ku yiwe enyangeni ngokwetuka ukuba ku bonwe into e um*h*lola; inyanga i tsho ukuti, "Loko e ni ku bonile Ubani, itongo lakwini. U ya zibonakalisa ngako. Bonga ni, ku muke."

sometimes a snake which is not an Itongo; perhaps an antelope comes to the house; the people then take divining-rods, and go to a diviner, being afraid because an omen has appeared; the diviner says, "That which ye have seen is So-and-so, the Itongo of your house. He reveals himself by it. Worship, that it may depart."

A lete izilwane kwowakwabo ukuti ka fe, loku e nga vumi uku wa nika into etile a wa i bizayo; noma ku nge njalo e lungisa, e ng' oni nganto kuwo; ku ya vela ububi kuye lo 'muntu. A s' azi uma kw enza njani ukuti a ti pela umuntu o *h*labisa njalonjalo amad*h*lozi, a banjwe inyoka, noma isilo, noma 'emuke namanzi, noma a kalakatele esiweni, noma a *h*latshwe umuntu enk*q*ineni, noma a *h*latshwe inkomo; lezi 'zinto zi m velele. Uma e se file, abantu aba seleyo ba buzane omunye nomunye, ba ti, "Au, pela, ini ukuba Ubani a fe, loku ngensuku zonke si d*h*la inyama yezinkabi kuye, noma imbuzi, noma imvu, noma utshwala? Loko konke ku be kw enza ni na? Si be si nga ti tina u bonga Amad*h*lozi akubo na? Ini ukuba a fe pezu kwaloko na? O, kanti, nobongayo k' enzi 'luto; nongabongiyo u ya kolisa. Nga se ku yekwa nje."

The Amatongo bring animals to some one belonging to the village that he may die, because he has not been willing to give them a certain thing which they demand; or on the contrary when he worships them, and has in nothing sinned against them; yet mischief befalls the man. We do not understand how it is that a man who constantly sacrifices to the Amadhlozi should be seized by a snake, or a leopard, or be carried away by a stream; or fall over a precipice, or be stabbed by a man in a hunt, or be gored by a bullock; these things happen to him. When he is dead, those who are living ask one another, saying, "Oh, then, how is it that So-and-so is dead, when we daily ate the flesh of bullocks at his house, or of goats or of sheep, or drank beer? What effect had all that? Did we not think he was worshipping the Amadhlozi of his people? How is it that he is dead notwithstanding? O, forsooth, the worshipper gains nothing by his worship; and the man who does not worship does well. Let it be left alone entirely."

uyena umfo wenu; si ya 'kuti, isifo nje."

La tshona ilanga, e sa ti kubu*h*lungu; kanti ukusengwa kwezinkomo wa ti, "Ngi pe ni ukud*h*la, ngi d*h*le." Ba buza abafazi bake, ba ti, "Ku njani na?" A ti, "Ni zwa ngi ti ni na?" Ba ti, "Si zwa u funa ukud*h*la."

A ti, "Amanga, banta bami; nami ngi zwa in*h*liziyo; ku nga ti ni nga ngi pa ukud*h*lana; ni nga ngi pi kakulu; ngi pe ni ingcozana; ke ngi zwe."

Ba mu pa abafazi bake, ba mu pa amasi. Wa ti, "Ni nga wa teli umkcaba kakulu; u tele ni u be muncinyane, ku be 'manzana, ku nga jii, ku tambe; ke ngi zwe uma ku sa 'uvuma uma kw e*h*le na sempinjeni na."

Ba mw enzela njengokutsho kwake; kwa ba 'manzi, ka kwa jia, kwa ba 'manzi. Ba mu nika, wa d*h*la. Kw' e*h*la loko 'kud*h*la, ku be ku nga sa vumi uma a ku d*h*le. Ka z' a d*h*la kakulu; wa d*h*la ingcozana; wa nika abantwana bake. Wa ti, "Ake ni ng' enzele utshwala, ng' omile." Ba bu tata utshwala, ba mu nika. B' etemba abafazi bake en*h*liziyweni zabo, be bona indoda yabo i

your brother; we will say it is a simple disease."

When the sun went down he was still complaining of pain; but at the time of milking the cows he said, "Give me some food, that I may eat." His wives asked how the pain was. He replied, "What do you hear me say?" They said, "We hear you asking for food."

He replied, "I don't know, my children; even I[18] feel an inclination for food; it is as though you might give me a little; do not give me much; give me a little; let me just try."

So his wives gave him amasi. He said, "Do not put much crushed corn in it; put a little only, that it may be waterish, and not thick—that it may be soft; let me just try if the disease will now allow it to descend by the swallow."

They did for him as he asked; the food was fluid, not thick. They gave him and he ate. He was able to swallow, although he had been unable to eat. He did not eat much; he ate a little; he gave his children. He said, "Just give me some beer; I am thirsty." They took beer and gave him. His wives had confidence in their hearts when they saw their husband

[18] *Nami*, even I who have been so ill.

funda ukud*hl*a; ba tokoza en*hl*iziyweni zabo, loku be be se be *hl*ezi be novalo ukuti, "Umakazi, ka ku d*hl*i nje ukud*hl*a, isifo sikulu?" Ba ba nokujabula en*hl*iziyweni; ka ba pumisela emlonyeni, ba bhekana kodwa ngame*hl*o. Wa bu puza utshwala, wa kcela uguai, wa ti, "Banta bami, ngi shiyele ni noguai, ke ngi beme." Ba m shiyela, loku noguai e be e nga sa m bemi. Abafazi bake ba bhekana, ba mangala ukubona umuntu e se bema uguai, loku id*hl*ozi li be li m vimbele na kuguai, e nga sa m bemi. Abafazi be pika en*hl*iziyweni zabo, ukuti, "Elinjani id*hl*ozi e se li m vimbele na kuguai na?" Ba be nokwesaba, be ti, "Isifo; a si lo itongo."

taking a mouthful of food; they rejoiced in their hearts, for they had been fearful, saying, "Is it then that the disease is great, since he does not eat?" They rejoiced in their hearts; they did not speak out their joy, but looked at each other only. He drank the beer, and asked for snuff, saying, "Give me some snuff too, my children; let me just take a little." They gave him some, for he had left off taking snuff too. His wives looked at each other, and wondered to see the man now taking snuff; for the Itongo had restrained him also from taking snuff. His wives had disputed in their hearts, saying, "What kind of an Itongo is this that restrains him even from snuff?" They were afraid, thinking it was disease and not an Itongo which was affecting him.

Wa m bema uguai, wa lala; u te uma a lale, bwa fika ubutongo, wa lala. U ti pakati kwamasuku wa fika umfo wabo, wa ti, "Mfo wetu, konje u tise izinkomo? u ya 'ku zi *hl*aba kusasa na?" Wa vuma oleleyo, wa ti, "Ehe, ngi ya 'ku i *hl*aba. Ini wena, mfo wetu, u ti kumina a ngi ze nga ku pata; zi be zonke izinkomo, ngi zi *hl*aba nje, ngi ku pate ngezibongo zako; ngokuba wa be u ik*q*awe, u *hl*abana?"

He took snuff, and lay down; and when he lay down, sleep came. And in the middle of the night his brother came and said, "So then, my brother, have you pointed out the cattle? will you kill them in the morning?" The sleeper assented, saying, "Yes, yes, I will kill one. Why do you, my brother, say to me I never call on you, whilst whenever I kill cattle I call on you by your laud-giving names; for you were a brave, and stabbed in the conflict?"

Wa ti, "Ehe; ngi tsho ngakona, ngi funa inyama. Mina pela se nga fa, nga ku shiya nomuzi; wa ba uomuzi omkulu."

He replied, "Yes, yes, I say it with reason, when I wish for flesh. I indeed died, and left you with a village;[19] you had a large village."

Wa ti, "Ehe, mfo wetu, wa ngi shiya nawo umuzi, wa ngi shiya nawo nje ke; wena wa fa, u zi k*q*edile ini izinkomo na?"

He said, "Yes, yes, my brother, you left me with a village; but when you left me with it, and died, had you killed all the cattle?"

Wa ti, "K*q*a, nga ngi nga zi k*q*edile."

He replied, "No, I had not killed them all."

A ti, "Po, wena kababa, u ti, mina ma ngi zi k*q*ede ini na?"

He said, "Well then, child of my father, do you tell me to destroy them all?"

A ti, "K*q*a, a ngi tsho ukuti, zi k*q*ede. Ngi ti, i kona ngi tanda uma umuzi wako u be mukulu."

He replied, "No, I do not tell you to destroy them all. But I tell you to kill, that your village may be great."

Wa papama. Wa ti uma a papame, w' ezwa 'se sindile; ubu*h*lungu o be bu sesikaleni, se bu pelile. Wa papama, wa vuka, wa *h*lala; wa mu zamazisa umfazi, wa ti, "Mwabani, vuka, u kanyise eziko." Wa vuka umfazi, wa vutela, wa kcataz' uguai, wa bema; wa buza umfazi, wa ti, "Ku njani na?" Wa ti, "Au, ak' u tule; ngi papama, umzimba wami se u lula; kade ngi kuluma nomfo wetu; ngi papama, se ngi sindile nje." Wa m bema uguai ezimpumulweni zake, wa lala ubutongo. La pinda la fika futi lona lo 'mfo wabo, id*h*lozi. Wa fika wa ti, "Au, se ngi ku sindisile. Inkomo zi *h*labe kusasa."

He awoke. When he awoke he felt that he was now well; the pain which was in his side being no longer there. He awoke, and sat up; he jogged his wife, and said, "So-and-so, awake, and light a fire." His wife awoke and blew up the fire; she poured snuff into her hand and took it, and asked him how he was. He replied, "Oh! just be quiet; on awaking my body was feeling light; I have been speaking with my brother; on awaking I was quite well." He took some snuff, and went to sleep. The Itongo of his brother came again. He came saying, "See, I have now cured you. Kill the cattle in the morning."

---

19 *Nga ku shiya nomuzi*, I left you with a village, that is, I died, leaving you to inherit the property which I possessed.

Kwa sa kusasa wa vuka, wa ngena esibayeni. Loko be kona abafo wabo abancinyane, wa ba biza, wa ngena esibayeni, nabo ba ngena abafo wabo esibayeni. Wa ti, "Ngi ni biza nje, se ngi sindile. Umfo wetu u t' u se ngi pilisile." Wa ti, "Kupula ni inkabi." Ba i kupula. Wa ti, "Kupula ni inyumbakazi leyo." Ba zi kupula zombili. Za fika pambi kwake enhla nesibaya, z' ema. Wa bonga, wa ti:—

"Ehe, yidhla ni, nina bakwiti. Idhloz' elihle, uma ku pile nezingane, imizimba i be mnandi! Ngi ti, ini wena ukuti u ng' umfo wetu, u da u ti u nga fika kumina ngi lele, ngi ku pupe, ngi be se ngi za 'kugula na? Idhlozi elihle eli fika kumuntu li kulume izindaba ezinhle. Indaba se ngi ya i kuluma, se ngi ya gula. Ezinjani izinkomo eziti zi dhliwa umninizo, zi be zi dhliwa ngokugula na? Ngi ti mina, Peza, ngi yeke uku ngi gulisa. Ngi ti, Fika kumina ngi lele, u ngi tshele indaba, u ti, 'Mfo wetu, ngi tanda ukuti.'—U ya fika kumina, u fika ngoku ngi bulala. Ku ya bonakala uma wa be umuntu o ishinga: u z' u be ishinga na ngapansi emhlabeni na?

In the morning he arose and went into the cattle-pen. But he had some younger brothers; he called them, and went into the pen, and his brothers went in with him. He said, "I just call you, for I am now well. My brother says he has now cured me." Then he told them to bring an ox. They brought it. He said, "Bring that barren cow." They brought them both. They both came to him to the upper part of the pen, and stood there. He prayed, saying:—

"Well then, eat, ye people of our house. Let a good Itongo be with us, that the very children may be well, and the people be in health! I ask, how is it that you, since you are my brother, come to me again and again in my sleep, and I dream of you, and am then sick? That Itongo is good which comes to a man and tells him good news. I am always complaining that I am constantly ill. What cattle are those which their owner devours, devouring them through being ill? I say, Cease; leave off making me ill. I say, Come to me when I am asleep, and tell me a matter, and say, My brother, I wish so-and-so.—You come to me, coming for the purpose of killing me. It is clear that you were a bad fellow when you were a man: are you still a bad fellow under the ground? I

Nga ngi nga ti mina, ku ya 'kuti itongo lako li fike ka*h*le kumina, li ngi tshele izindaba. Ini wena, u ng' umfo wetu omkulu wokulungisa umuzi, ku nga veli indaba embi ngapakati kwomuzi, ngoba mina ng' azi ukuti u ng' umnikaziwo?"

used not to think that your Itongo would come to me with kindness, and tell me good news. How is it that you come with evil, you, my eldest brother, who ought to bring good to the village, that no evil might come to it, for I know that you are its owner?"

U teta nazo ke, u ya bonga, e ti:—

He says these words about the cattle, and returns thanks, saying:—

"Nazi izinkomo e ngi ku nika zona—nansi inkabi ebomvu, nansi inyumbakazi encokazi. Zi *h*labe. Mina ngi ti, Indaba ngi tshele ka*h*le, ngi vuke umzimba wami umnandi. Ngi ti, A ba pelele bonke abakwiti, ba butane lapa kuwena, wena u tanda inyama."

"There are the cattle which I offer you—there is a red ox, there is a red and white barren cow. Kill them. I say, Tell me a matter kindly, that on awaking my body may be free from pain. I say, Let all the Amatongo of the people of our house come here together to you, you who are fond of meat."

A be se ti ke, "Zi gwaze ni." A u tate umkonto omunye umfo wabo, a be se i gwaza inyumbakazi, i we pansi. A i gwaze inkabi; zi bod*h*le zombili; a zi bulale, zi fe. A ti, "Zi *h*linze ni." Ba zi *h*linze ke; zi pele izikumba; ba i d*h*le ke esibayeni. Amadoda e butene onke e zokcela inyama; a w esuse ngezito; a d*h*le, 'esute, a bonge, a ti, "Si ya bonga, wena kabani. Si kulekela id*h*lozi eli*h*le. Uma si bone pela, uma, bala, id*h*lozi eligulisayo, si ya 'ubona ukuti, bala, i lona ishinga eli umfo

And then he says, "Stab them." One of his brothers takes an assagai, and stabs the barren cow; it falls down. He stabs the ox; both bellow; he kills them—they die. He tells them to skin them. So they skin them; the hides are taken off; they eat them in the cattle-pen. All the men assemble to ask for food; they take it away joint by joint; they eat and are satisfied, and give thanks, saying, "We thank you, Son of So-and-so. We pray that the Itongo may be propitious. When we see indeed that it is an Itongo which makes you ill, we shall see that that Itongo

wenu. Si be si ng' azi uma inyama si za 'ku i dhla nawe ngokugula kwako okukulu kangaka. Si ya bona ukuti leli ishinga li ya ku bulala; se si y' etokoza ke ngokuba si ku bona u pilile."

UGUAISE MDUNGA.

is the wretch which is your brother. We did not know if we should eat meat with you through your very severe illness. We now see it is the wretch which is killing you; and so we now are glad because we see you are well."

The Amatongo are felt in the Shoulders.

AMAHLOMBE omuntu o inyanga indawo yokuzwa. Konke a ku zwayo ku vela kuleyo 'ndawo yamahlombe. Amahlombe indawo yamatongo kubantu aba izinyanga. Uma umuntu o inyanga e bambelwa omunye u ya zonda; ngoku m pata lapo ku nga ti u m gwaza ngomkonto; u y' ezwa masinyane njengokungati ku kona isilonda. Nabanye aba nge 'nyanga a ba vumi ukubanjelwa emahlombe; ngokuba ba ti ku kona oku ba hlupayo ngokubanjelwa. Futi uma umuntu 'emi emva kwenyanga i ya m susa masinyane ngokuti, "Suka, u ya ng' apula; njengokungati u hlezi pezu kwami."

Lapa si ti, a li ko itongo kuyena emzimbeni, si kuluma ngokuba o be ku tshiwo, ku tiwa ku funwa amatongo, se kw enziwe; kepa ukufa ku ng' esuki; si ti ke, ka natongo; a li ko itongo kuye.

THE sensitive part with a doctor is his shoulders. Every thing he feels is in the situation of his shoulders. That is the place where black men feel the Amatongo. If a doctor is touched by another person he is in pain; if he touches him there it is as if he stabbed him with an assagai; he feels at once as though there was a sore place there. And others who are not doctors do not allow another to take hold of them by the shoulders; for they say it causes them pain to be laid hold of. And if a man stands behind a doctor he makes him go away directly, saying, "Get away, you are hurting me; it is as if you sat upon me."

When we say there is not an Itongo in his body, we say so because when that has been done which it was said the Amatongo wished, the disease remains; therefore we say, he has no Itongo; there is not an Itongo in him.

Laying the Itongo, or Spirit.

Ku ya bizwa inyanga uma ku kona umuntu o gulayo, kepa e katazwa umuntu emunye. Ku ti a nga m pupa lowo 'muntu owa fayo, umzimba wake u nga lungi; ku se e wa lauza lawo 'mapupo ngokuti, "Au, ngi ya *h*lupeka. Uma ku fika ubani ebusuku ngi lele, umzimba wami a u lungi. Ngi ko*h*liwe ukuba ngi nga ze ng' enze njani."

Kepa uma nembala loko 'ku m pupa kwake se ku m gulisa, ku bizwe inyanga e za 'ku m vimba. I ti, "Bheka ke; a ko ti ngam*h*la u m pupayo, u tate lo 'muti, u u d*h*le; u tate netshe noma isikuni, u si fele ngalawo 'mate e u m pupe e semlonyeni ngoku*h*langanisa amate na lo 'muti; u wa fele esikunini, noma itshe; u si jigijele nyovane u nga bheki. Uma u bheka a ya 'kubuya lawo 'mapupo." Nembala 'enze njalo.

I loko ke ukwelatshwa kwepupa. Uma ku d*h*lula, amapupa e buya futi, inyanga y enze okunye, i li vimbe lelo 'pupa lalowo 'muntu. Ku tatwe umuti o *h*langaniswe neminye ngokwedukisa ukuba a nga be e sa m bona. A ye 'ku

A DOCTOR is summoned when a man is ill, he being troubled by one man.[20] He dreams perhaps of the dead man, and then has pain in his body; in the morning he tells others his dreams. He says, "O, I am troubled. When So-and-so comes to me by night, my body is in pain. I cannot tell what to do."

And if his dreaming makes him ill, they summon a doctor to come and close up the way against him. The doctor says to him, "Look; when you dream of him, take this medicine and chew it; then take a stone or a piece of firewood, and spit on it the spittle which is in your mouth when you dream of him, mixed with this medicine; spit it either on a piece of firewood or on a stone; and throw it behind your back without looking. If you look the dreams will recur." And he does so.

This is the way dreaming is treated. If the thing goes on, and the dreams come back again, the doctor adopts another plan of treatment, and closes the way against the man's dream. Several medicines are mixed together for the purpose of misleading the Itongo, that he may see it no more. He goes to a distance to shut him

[20] That is, one of the Amatongo.

m vimba kude, noma esidulini; loko a ku peteyo a ku fake kona, a goduke ke, a nga be e sa bheka ngemuva.

Ku njalo kubantu abamnyama. Ku tiwa, "Id*h*lozi eli katazayo uma li gulisa abantu ngoku li bona, li ya vinjwa." Kakulu lezi 'zinto zoku*h*lupa umuntu zi vela kwabesifazana aba felwe amadoda, ba ngenwe abafo wabo, kumbe abanye abantu. Kepa itongo lalo 'muntu o fileyo li ya landela njalonjalo umfazi wake. Ku ti uma e se e miti, uma li fika itongo lake, a be se u ya gula, si ze si pume leso 'sisu; ku ze ku vele nokuba li vinjwe ngaloko 'kwenza kwalo.

Uma li m *h*lupa e kwenye indoda e nga ngenwanga; uma lowo 'mfazi wa shiya abantwana baleyo 'ndoda efileyo, efileyo i ya m landa ngokuti kuye, "Abanta bami wa ba shiya kubani na? U zokwenza ni lapa na? Buyela kubanta bami. Uma u nga vumi, ngi za 'ku ku bulala." Li vinjwe masinyane kulowo 'muzi ngoku*h*lupa lowo 'wesifazana.

Kumbe elinye nembala a ze a buye kulowo 'mendo wake, a nga be e s' enda, a buyele ekaya, a ye 'kulonda abantwana. Ku tiwe wa buyiswa uyise wabantwana. Ku njalo ke ukuvimba itongo izinyanga.

UMPENGULA MBANDA.

up there, perhaps in an ant-heap; what he has in his hand he puts into the heap, and goes home, and he never sees it again.

Such is the custom with black men. It is said, "A troublesome spirit which appears to a man and makes him ill, is laid." These troublesome things occur most commonly in women who have lost their husbands, and are taken to wife by his brothers or by others. But the spirit of the dead husband follows the wife continually. If she is pregnant, and the spirit of her husband comes to her, and she is ill and miscarries; the Itongo is at length laid because it has acted thus.

If it trouble her when she has gone to another man without being as yet married; if she has left her husband's children behind, the dead husband follows her and asks, "With whom have you left my children? What are you going to do here? Go back to my children. If you do not assent I will kill you." The spirit is at once laid in that village because it harasses the woman.

Perhaps another spirit never leaves her until she returns to the village of her dead husband; she never marries again, but remains at home and takes care of her children. It is said the children's father brought her back again. This is how doctors lay a spirit.

The Amatongo reveal Medicines, &c., in dreams.

NGESINYE isikati kubantu abapata imiti ba y' a*h*lukanisa imiti yabo nemiti a ba i boniswa aba nga se ko. Njengaloku Undayeni u b' e kolise ukwazi imiti enjalo: ku tiwe kuye ebusuku, "Hamba, u ye endaweni etile, u fike u mbe umuti otile; lowo 'muti w elapa ukufa okutile." Undayeni wa e nemiti kakulu enjalo a i boniswa abakubo e lele. Leyo 'miti wa y a*h*lukanisa, nemiti a y aziyo na leyo 'miti a i boniswayo.

SOMETIMES men who have medicines distinguish between their own medicines, and those they have been shown by the dead. For instance, Undayeni was frequently given the knowledge of such medicines: it used to be said to him in a dream, "Go to such a place, and when you get there dig up a certain medicine; that medicine is the remedy for a certain disease." Undayeni had very many such medicines, which he was shown by the spirits of his people whilst he slept. He made a distinction between the medicines he knew, and the medicines which were revealed to him.

Futi a ku si ye yedwa kuloko. Baningi. Ngi be ngi ke ngi bone nobaba futi, Unkomid*h*lilale; lokupela u be inyanga enkulu yokwelapa izinkomo uma zi fa; futi e inyanga neyemiti. Ngi be ngi hamba naye uma e bizwa umuntu, ku fa izinkomo zake lowo 'muntu. Ngi zwe e se ngi tshela lapa si mba imiti, u ti, "Yimba lo 'muti; ngi u piwe ebusuku; kwa tiwa, ngi ya 'ku u *h*langanisa nemiti etile." Nembala ke kwa ba njalo;

And Undayeni was not alone in this respect. There are many like him. I have seen my father also, Unkomidhlilale;[21] for he was a great cattle doctor; and he also had many medicines for men. I used to go with him when he was called by any one whose cattle were ill. I heard him say as we were digging up medicines, "Dig up that; I had that revealed to me in a dream; I was told to mix it with certain other medicines." And so it was continually; there

[21] *U-nkom'-i-dhl'-i-lale*, The-bullock-which-eats-and-lies-down. Implying that as a bullock in abundant pastures eats and lies down, so he shall have abundance of food and freedom from care,—that he shall "dwell in a large pasture."

a ku pelanga loko 'kupupa imiti; wa ze wa ba nemiti eminingi. Ngako loko izinkomo uma zi fa u be e zi siza, a z' elape, a zi uqumisela ilanga li be linye, a ti, "A zi nga wa puzi amanzi; a zo puza intelezi ku be ukupela." Nembala ku bekwa imbiza enkulu esibayeni, i gcwale imiti namanzi; lapo amanzi e se kcwebile, imiti i buyele ngapansi, zi puze ezinye; ezinye zi banjwe zi puziswe. Ku ti ngamhla e se zi nika amanzi, ku letwe leyo 'miti, ku yiwe emfuleni nayo, a fike a i tele emanzini, zi puze ngenzansi izinkomo.

U ke wa zi dhla izinkomo zabantu ngaloko 'kwelapa kwake. Wa duma wa ba inyanga. Uma za sinda lezo 'zinkomo, u se u puma nenkomo pakati kwazo. Uma e fika, ku kona e se zi lele pansi, a ti, "I nga fa le. Ngi ya 'kuba ng' ahlulekile." Nembala a zi vuse, a ngene pakati kwazo kusihlwa e pete isihlanti, e mumata amafuta, a si vutele isihlanti pakati kwezinkomo. Izinkomo z' etuke kakulu zi bona ilangabi elisabekayo e gijima nesibaya sonke a kqede; a ti, "Ku nga buye ngi zwe, ku tiwa i kona inkomo e sale ya fa, ni nga be ni s' eza kumi; ku ya 'kuba ng' ahlulekile."

was no end of his dreaming of medicines, until he had a great many. Therefore he was useful to cattle when they were ill; he gave them physic; he ordered them for one day to drink no water, but only that into which he had put his medicines. And a large pot was put in the cattle-pen full of medicines and water; when the medicines had sunk to the bottom and the water was clear, some drank; others were drenched. When they were allowed to drink water, the medicines were taken to the river and put into the water, and the cattle drank lower down.

He obtained many cattle from people for doctoring their cattle. He became a celebrated doctor. If the cattle got well he had one given him. If when he came some were lying down, he said, "That one may die. [But if it die] I shall cure none of them." And so he roused them up, going into the midst of them in the evening, carrying in his hand a torch, pouring fat on it, and kindling it when in the midst of the cattle. The cattle were much frightened when they saw the great flame, as he ran through the whole cattle-pen; and he said, "If I hear that one of these cattle has died, never come to me again; I shall not be able to do anything."

Ngesinye isikati ku kona umuntu o hamba ngasese komunye e nga m boni; kepa omunye e ng' azi 'luto ngaye lowo 'muntu, e umngane wake. Kepa uma w' ezwa ebusuku ukuti, "Ubani lo u m enza umngane wako nje. A u boni ini ukuba u ya 'ku ku bulala na? U ti ku ngani uma u ti u ti?" (e tsho indaba,) nembala lowo 'muntu u ya 'ku i kumbula ukuti, "Hau. Nembala, uma ku njalo Ubani a nga ngi zonda ngendaba leyo." A k*q*ale ukupuma kuye ngoku m k*x*waya. Kepa lelo 'pupa u ya 'ku li lauza, a ti, "Ngi ya mangala uma ngi bone Ubani e ngi bulala ngendaba etile." U se hambele kude naye. Noma lowo e ti, "Bani, manje wa hambela kude nami. Ini na? Si pambene ngani?" Kepa lowo u ya 'ku m pendula ngezwi loku m dukisa ngokuti, "O, wena kabani, kanti u ti nga ba ku kona indaba e ngi pambene nawe ngayo na? K*q*a. A ku ko 'luto. Ngi libaziswa ukutinitini, kupela," e tsho izinbangcabangca nje.

UMPENGULA MBANDA.

Sometimes there is a man who is acting with a secret intention of injuring another without his suspecting it, and without his knowing any thing about him, he being his friend. But if he hears in a dream a voice saying to him, "So-and-so is pretending merely to be your friend. Do you not see that he will kill you? What do you think he means by saying such and such things?" (alluding to something he has said), he remembers it and exclaims, "Yes, surely. So-and-so may hate me on that account." And he begins to separate from him and to be on his guard. And he tells the dream and says, "I wonder that I have seen So-and-so killing me about such and such a matter." And he keeps at a distance from him. And if he says to him, "So-and-so, now you keep at a distance from me. What is it? What difference has arisen between us?" the other puts him off by saying, "O, Son of So-and-so, can you think there is any thing which has made me quarrel with you? No. There is nothing. I am occupied with such and such concerns. That is all," saying what is really mere subterfuge.

A man's Itongo resembles him in character.

UNJIKIZA kakcuba, Und*h*lebekazizwa, Unotshelwaezitshela, kwa ku ik*q*awe elikulu e namand*h*la kakulu, e nomzimba omkulu; ku isijak*q*aba sendoda e lukuni; e sukile e u dedele um*h*laba.

Kwa ti kwancolosi lapa a e konza kona, kwa fika Amazulu e ishumi e hamba e bulala lapa e tunyelwe kona. Kepa a nga yi ngomteto wenkosi; a zenzele pakati kwemizi lap' e nga tunyelwe kona, a pate kabi abantu, e d*h*la 'magula nokud*h*la ngokuti, "Loku si abantu bakomkulu, amapand*h*le a ya 'kubaleka si sa vela nje. Ubani wasemapand*h*leni o ya 'kuya kwomkulu, a ye 'ku si mangalela na? Si ya 'kuzenzela nje, si diye ngefusi letu." Nembala ke

UNJIKIZA, the son of Ukcuba, Undhlebekazizwa,[22] Unotshelwaezitshela,[23] was a celebrated brave, of great strength, and huge body; all his muscles were prominent and hard; and his head was high above the ground.[24]

It happened among the Amancolosi with whom he was living, that there came the Amazulu going and killing wherever they were sent. But they did not act in accordance with the chief's law, but acted after their own heart in villages to which they had not been sent, treating the people cruelly, eating their milk and other food, saying, "Since we are the people of the chief, the rustics will fly as soon as they see us. Who among them will lay a charge against us before the chief? We will do just as we like, and set ourselves our own limit."[25] And

[22] *U-nd*hlebe-*ka-zi-zwa*, He-is-ears-which-hear-not, or The-ears-which-hear-not-man. Implying a man who refuses to listen to any counsel or explanation, but at once attempts to conclude a matter by fighting.

[23] *U-notshelwa-e-zi-tshela*, When-he-has-been-told-he-tells-the-news. That is, he pays no attention whatever to what is said to him, but at once gives his own account of the matter, and insists upon his own opinion.—These two names are izibongo given to him on account of his character.

[24] That is, he was very tall.

[25] This is a proverbial saying. "You shall set for yourself your own limit at my village,"—that is, you shall do just as you like.

'enza njalo, a z' a fika kwowakiti umuzi. A fika kwa 'besifazana bodwa, ku nge ko 'mlisa. A zenzela ekud*h*leni, a kalisa abantwana e b' amuka ukud*h*la, nabesifazana ba kala be ti, "Uma u kona Und*h*lebekazizwa nga ni ng' enzi nje. Yenza ni belu; u za 'ufika."

indeed they acted thus, until they came to our village. When they came, there were none there but women; there was not a single man there. They did as they liked with the food; they made the children cry by taking away what they were eating; and the women cried saying, "If Undhlebekazizwa were here, you would not do so. Go on then; he will be here presently."

Nembala kwa ti ku 'sikati wa fika, w' ezwa umsindo wokukala e sesangweni. Wa tshaya ngewisa lake elikulu, e ti, "U lambile ke Unod*h*lolamazibuko. U za 'kwesuta ke nam*h*la."

And indeed after a time he came, and heard the noise of crying whilst he was at the gateway. He smote the ground with his huge club, saying, "Unothlolamazibuko is hungry.[26] It shall have its fill to-day."

[26] *U-nothlola-mazibuko.* The name of his club. It means, He-who-watches-the-fords, that is, to prevent an enemy crossing to do damage.—There is a terrible threat in his words.—It is common for braves among the natives to give names to their clubs, spears, &c. Thus, one calls his assagai which he uses for the purpose of getting food for his household *U-simbela-banta-bami*, He-digs-up-for-my-children. Another calls his *Imbubuzi*, The-groan-causer, because when it stabs men or cattle their groans are heard. *Igumgehle*, the glutton, is the name of a club, because when used in fighting, the opponents are destroyed with as much rapidity as a glutton swallows his food. *U-silo-si-lambile*, the name of an assagai, meaning the-hungry-leopard, is so called because its owner attacks the enemy like a hungry leopard. *U-dhl'-ebusuku*, The-eater-in-the-dark; the name of a club, so called because it is used to destroy secretly and by stealth; the owner of it coming on his victims by night, or rushing on them from an ambush.

This custom of naming their choice weapons is met with among other people in olden times. Thus Arthur commenced his career of greatness by obtaining the miraculous sword Escalibore, which could

"Kerve steel, and yren, and al thing."

(Ellis's Specimens. Vol. I., p. 243.) He gave names also to his shield, sword, and spear. Thus:—"Over his shoulders he threw his shield called Priwen, on which a picture of holy Mary, mother of God, constantly recalled her to his memory. Girt with Caliburn, a

'Ezwa Amazulu; lokupela a ya m azi; kwa ti nya umsindo. A puma ngokunyiba, e baleka, 'emuka. Kwa ti kusa a e banjwa kwomunye umuzi ngokuhlupa kwawo; a botshwa, a yiswa emhumeni, a ngeniswa kona. Wa ti Undhlebekazizwa, "A ba tshiswe, ku gaulwe izinkuni." Ba ngena emhumeni, kwa fakwa izinkuni, kwa baswa umlilo, kwa bebezelwa ngamahhau, kwa ngeniswa umusi. Ba futelana, ba fa bonke. Ku ze ku be namhla nje a kw aziwa kwazulu ukuba ba ya ngapi na.

The Amazulu heard; for they know him; the noise was at once hushed; and they went out stealthily and fled away. In the morning they were caught at another village because of the trouble they gave; they were bound and carried to a den and confined in it. Undhlebekazizwa told the people to fetch firewood and burn them. The people went into the cave and put down the firewood and lit a fire, and fanned it with their shields, and drove the smoke into the cave. They were unable to breathe, and all died. And it is not known to this day by the Amazulu what became of them.[27]

Kwa ti ke ekukcitekeni kwezwe li kcitwa Amazulu, kwa balekwa, kwa ngenwa emahlatini nezinkomo. A zi fumana zakwiti. Ya hlabana, y' ahlulwa yakwiti; kwa sala yena Undhlebekazizwa. A ti Amazulu, "Namhla ku namuhla! Si ya 'ubona ukuba u za 'u s' ahlula na. Loku kade u si hlupa, nza si suke si hambele emapandhleni." Ba m hlaba ngemikonto kulelo 'hlati. Wa bulala amashumi ama-

It happened when the land was desolated by the Amazulu, the people fled into the forests with their cattle. The Amazulu found ours. We fought with them, but our people were conquered; and Undhlebekazizwa alone remained. The Amazulu said, "To-day is to-day! We shall see if you will conquer us. For for a long time you have plagued us when we have gone to the outer districts." They stabbed him with their assagais in the forest. He

most excellent sword, and fabricated in the isle of Avalon, he graced his right hand with the lance named Ron. This was a long and broad spear, well contrived for slaughter." (*Id.*, *p.* 60.)—Roland had his terrible sword Durindale. (*Id. Vol. II.*, *p.* 304.) Otuel, the Saracen champion, had his sword Corrouge. (*Id.*, *p.* 317.) Charlemagne had his good sword Joyeuse. (*Id.*, *p.* 346.)

[27] That is, the matter was kept a secret, and the Amazulu did not know what had become of their soldiers.

bili. Wa ti, "Ngi bulale ni ke manje. Se ngi zend*h*lalele. Ngi za 'kulala pezu kwabantu." Ba m gwaza indawo zonke zomzimba. Kwa ba njengokumila kwom*h*langa imikonto emzimbeni. Wa pela ke. I leyo ke indaba yake.

Isilo u be si bambisa kwengane nje e yedwa e*h*latini; a hambe e kala njengengane, e gak*q*a ngamadolo. Isilo si fike kuye, si kwele, a si tate njengempukane, a si bulale.

U be sabeka. U be nge naluto lo 'muntu lu lu*h*le e *h*langane naye end*h*leleni, u be m bulala, a tate loko a ku tandayo. Ba jabula abaningi ngokufa kwake, ngokuba wa e *h*lupa kakulu; konke u be kw enza ngen*h*luzula; inyewe ya i nge ko. Ik*c*ala li be li nga tetwa emzini wakwiti e se kona; u be li k*q*eda ngenduku. Li tetwe e nge ko; e kona k*q*a. Ku njalo ke.

Nctongo lake libi. Ka patwa na nam*h*la njc emzini wakwiti. Uma ku kona o m patayo, u tuliswa masinyane, ku tiwe, "Ka patwa lowo pakati kwomuzi. A nga u bubisa." U patwa ngam*h*la kw enziwe ukud*h*la kupela. Ka patwa ezindabeni.

UMPENGULA MBANDA.

killed twenty of them. He then said, "Kill me now. I have now spread out a mat for myself to lie on. I shall lie on men." They stabbed him in every part of his body. Their spears stuck in him as thick as reeds in a morass. So he died. This is his history.

He would lay hold of a leopard by himself in the forest, as though it was a mere child; he would go along crying like a child, crawling on his knees. The leopard would leap on him, and he seize it as though it was a fly and kill it.

He was much dreaded. Every one who had any thing pretty whom he met with in the way, he would kill and take what he liked. Many were glad at his death, for he gave much trouble, and did every thing in an arbitrary way; he had no patience. No matter was discussed in our village when he was there; he would bring it to a conclusion with a stick. It was discussed when he was absent, but not when he was at home.

And his Itongo is wicked. His name is never mentioned to this day in our village. If any one mentions him, he is at once silenced, and told not to mention his name in the village, for he might destroy it. He is mentioned only when any cattle are killed. He is not mentioned at other times.[23]

---

[23] This modern Samson has all the characteristics of the cham-

A Doctor of Medicine deceived by the Itongo.

Ku te ngezinsukwana ezi d*h*lulileyo, kwa ku kona umuntu emakuzeni; w ake en*h*lavini ngakusigwili kamsengana. Lowo 'muntu u inyanga yemiti. W' esuka kumahaule ngeminyaka ed*h*lulileyo; u yena Omahaule nomazwana nofaku ba pambana ngaye, ukuze ba kcitane nje. Umahaule wa m k*x*otsha; kepa Umazwana nofaku ba m pikela, ngokuba umukwe kamazwana; igama lake Un*q*an*q*aza. Wa fika ke lapa emakuzeni kusigwili, w' aka.

Naku ku ti ngam*h*la ku vela ukufa okukulu kwembo, se ku ngene kwasigwili, kwa susa abantu ababili. Usigwili e nga ka bi nakcala, wa fika ke Un*q*an*q*aza e pete umuti; wa ti kusigwili, "Sigwili, ngi za lapa nje kuwe, ngi letwa itongo; li ti, a ngi zoku kw elapa." Usigwili lowo isidukwane lapa emakuzeni, kubo inkosana kwambanjwa, mukulu kutoi lo kwabakambanjwa.

A LITTLE while ago there was a man among the Amakuza; he lived on the Inthlavini near Usigwili, the son of Umsengana. He was a doctor of medicine. Some years ago he left Umahaule; it is he on account of whom Umahaule quarrelled with Umazwana and Ufaku, until they separated one from the other. Umahaule drove him away, and they defended him, for he is Umazwana's father-in-law; his name is Un*q*an*q*aza. So he came here among the Amakuza, and lived with Usigwili.

At the time when severe epidemic dysentery prevailed, and attacked the household of Usigwili, it carried off two people. Whilst Usigwili was as yet free from disease, Un*q*an*q*aza came to him with medicines, and said to him, "Usigwili, I come to you because the Itongo told me to come and treat you." That Usigwili is a great man here among the Amakuza; among his own people, the house of Umbanjwa,[29] he is a petty chief, the elder brother of Utoi among the descendants of Umbanjwa.

---

pions of old legends. It is difficult to conceive such a description as is here given to refer to a man of a generation just passed away. He was the uncle of the narrator.

[29] Umbanjwa, the Unkulunkulu of that family.

Usigwili naye wa y azi indaba yetongo, wa kolwa; ka buzanga ukuti, "Ku ngani uma itongo li ze kuwe, n*q*an*q*aza, li nga tsheli mina ukuba ngi za 'ugula, ngi fanele ng' elatshwe masinyane uwe?" Ka buza 'luto ngaleso 'sikati ngovalo lokuba nembala id*h*lozi li k*q*inisile; loku impi naku se i ngene emzini wami ukufa.

Usigwili too knew what the Itongo had said,[30] and believed; and so did not ask, "How is it that the Itongo comes to you, Un*q*an*q*aza, without telling me that I am about to be ill, and it is proper that I at once put myself under your care?" He asked no question at the time because he was afraid that the Itongo had spoken the truth, and said, "See, death has come like an army into my village."

Wa vumela pezulu ukuti, "Yebo, yelapa." Lokupela lo 'muntu u y' etembeka ngobunyanga bake. Wa ko*h*lwa ukuba kumahaule u k*x*otshwe ngokutakata: ngoku m pikela kwabo kwa fipaza ukukcabanga kwake ngaloko 'kutukwa kwake. Wa u puza ke umuti lowo. Wa ti, "Ngi ku puziso wona nje; u ya 'upuma ngend*h*lela e ngapansi, a u z' ukubuya ngengapezulu; u ya 'kuya ngengapansi." Kepa umuti wa pambana nokutsho kwake. Wa hamba ngend*h*lela zombili nengapansi; wa k*q*inisa kuzo zombili; wa tsho ngapezulu na ngapansi; kwa k*q*ina kwa ti nk*q*i loko 'kuhamba kwawo.

He assented at once, saying, "Yes, take me under your care." For the man is trusted much for his knowledge of disease. He forgot that he was driven from Umahaule's tribe for sorcery: because he had been defended by Umazwana and Ufaku, he had no thought of the bad name which he had had. So he drank the medicine. Un*q*an*q*aza said, "I give you this medicine; it will act as an aperient, not as an emetic." But the medicine did not act in accordance with his word. It acted both as a purge and an emetic in an excessive degree.

Se be twal' ame*h*lo, ba ti, "N*q*an*q*aza, lungisa; umuntu wa

The people now began to stare, and said, "Un*q*an*q*aza, correct the effects of your medicine; is the man dead whilst you are looking

[30] He knew because he too had dreamed a dream similar to that of Un*q*an*q*aza.

fa na?" Kepa u se ko*h*liwe noku u buyisa umuti wake, u s' a*h*luleka; u se putuzela; ka sa k*q*ondi a kw enzayo. Umuti lowo se u ukufa; u se u funa ukutabata isidumbu.

at him?"[31] But he was now unable to regulate the action of his medicine; he was quite beaten; and acted without reason, no longer knowing what to do. The medicine became poison, and now wished to take away the dead body.[32]

Se ku mangelwe ngaloko 'kwenza kukaun*q*an*q*aza. Nam*h*la leso 'situko sokuti u umtakati si ya kula kubo bonke, ukuti, "Nembala, ubani o nga ti ku nga gulwa e nga biziwe, a zibize na? Umtakati impela."

People began to wonder at what Un*q*an*q*aza had done. And now the word which pronounced him a sorcerer is heard every where, and people say, "Who ever went to a man who was not ill, without being called by him, of his own accord to treat him for disease? He is indeed a sorcerer."

Ku se njalo ke. A kw aziwa uma i za 'uzala 'nkonyana ni na.

UMPENGULA MBANDA.

Thus the matter stands at present. We do not know what the result will be.[33]

How the Amatongo are worshipped.

ITONGO kakulu li vama ukuzibonakalisa kwalo li ngena ngomuntu, li m bambe endaweni etile yomzimba, a be se u ya gula. Kepa ku tiwe, "Bani, u njenje, u nani na?"

THE Itongo for the most part when it reveals itself enters a village through some individual living there, and seizes on some part of his body, and so he is ill. And his friends ask him, "So-and-so, since you are in such a state, what is the matter with you?" He

31 "Umuntu wa fa na?"—We cannot render this literally. The saying casts the responsibility of death, if it takes place, on Un*q*an*q*aza.

32 Medicine is here personified. The medicine is now Death; and is working for the purpose of getting a corpse.

33 Lit., It is not yet known what calf the cow will bring forth. A proverbial saying.—This account was given to me in 1865. Usigwili died. And Un*q*an*q*aza died soon after, probably privately murdered.

A ti, "O, nam*h*la nje a ngi tokozi, ngi vuka umzimba wami u shiyene; ku zonde kakulu kuleyo 'ndawo." A bonakale noma e zik*q*inisa ukuti, "K*q*a, lo 'muntu, noma e zik*q*inisa, u ya fa; si ya m bona."

replies, "O, to-day I am not happy, having woke with my body well in one part and unwell in another;[34] it is very painful in this place." And it is clear that he is ill, though he makes the best of it, and they say, "No, the man, though he makes the best of it, is ill; we see that he is not well."

Kepa ngoku nga peli masinyane loko 'kufa, ku ze ku yiwe enyangeni yokubula. I fike inyanga, i ku tsho loko a gula iko. Kanti naye lowo 'muntu o gulayo ka tshongo 'luto ngaloko 'kufa; ngokuba ku vama ukuba labo 'bantu, noma be pupile, kwa sa umzimba ubu*h*lungu, a ba tandi ukuveza indaba bona; ngokuba kubantu abamnyama uku*h*laba izinkomo kw ande kakulu, kwa tiwa zi bizwa id*h*lozi; kepa ku buye ku tiwe kwomunye, "Hai! loku ku s' and' uku*h*latshwa, id*h*lozi eli ti ni

And because the disease does not cease at once they at length go to the diviner. The diviner comes and tells them the cause of the illness. But the sick man himself had said nothing about his illness; for it is generally the case that such people, although they have dreamed and in the morning awoke in pain, do not like to talk about it themselves; for among black men slaughtering cattle has become much more common than formerly, on the ground that the Idhlozi has demanded them; but they make reply to one who says so, "No! since a bullock has just been slaughtered, what does the Itongo say?[35] O, people are

34 "Umzimba wami u shiyene."—Lit., My body has left itself,—is affected differently in different parts. "Amasimu a ya shiyana," The fields are not all ripe at the same time. "Obani ba shiyene," Those men have gone one farther than the other.

35 "Id*h*lozi eli ti ni na?"—This Zulu idiom, which places the relative in the interrogative sentence, implies what cannot be expressed in a translation, that the person who asks the question does not believe that the Idhlozi has said any thing.—Id*h*lozi li ti ni na? is a simple enquiry for information.—Again, a person may say, Abantu a ba ka pelele, The people have not yet all arrived. If a man replies, O pi na o nge ko? Who is absent? it is understood at once that he sees that all are present; and the person who asserted that they were not

leli? O, abantu se be tanda inyama nje, umuntu a ti, 'Ngi pupe id*h*lozi,' kanti w enzela ukuze a d*h*le inyama." Kepa loko ku nga tshiwo obala, ku tshiwo ngasese. Ku ngaloko ke abantu be nga sa tsho ukuti, "Ngi gula nje, ngi pupe id*h*lozi." Se be yeka, ngokuti, "O, lo zi kona izinyanga ezi ya 'kutsho na loko e ngi ku bonileyo." Noma e buzwa ku tiwa, "Ku bonanga 'luto ekulaleni kwako na?" Kepa a landule. Kanti w' a*h*luleka ukuti itongo li biza inkomo, a ti, a ku nga pumi emlonyeni wake loko. A ku pume enyangeni.

now very fond of meat, and a man says he has dreamed of the Idhlozi, and forsooth he says so because he would eat meat." But this is not said openly, but secretly. Therefore a man no longer says, "I am ill. I have dreamed of the Idhlozi." They have left off saying so, and a man says, "O, since there are diviners who will say what I have seen," [why should I say any thing?] And even though they ask him, "Have you not seen something in your sleep?" he denies. For he is unable to say that the Itongo demands a bullock, determining not to mention such a thing; but to let the diviner mention it.

Ngokuba itongo a li bambi umninimuzi yedwa; li bamba nabantu nje bomuzi. Kepa umuntu nje, e nge si ye umninimuzi, ka namand*h*la okuti, "Ku tiwa abapansi, 'A ku *h*latshwe.'" Umninimuzi yedwa o nga yi 'kuvuma, uma ku banjwe yena ngesifo, ukuti a ku yiwe enyangeni; u ya 'kuti yena, noma ku patwa inyanga, a landule, a ti, "Ai! Ngi zwile. Hlaba ni inkomo etile; ngi za 'ululama." Ngokuba yena izinkomo ezake nomuzi owake; kubantwana bake a

For the Itongo does not choose the head of a village only, but also common people. But a mere man who is not the head of a village is not able to say, "The Amatongo command a bullock to be slaughtered." It is the head of the village alone who, if he is seized by disease, will not allow them to go to the diviner; if a diviner is mentioned, he will refuse, saying, "No! I have heard. Kill such and such a bullock, and I shall get well." For the cattle and the village are his; there are none among his children who can

all there looks again, and says, Nembala, So they are. If he says, Umu pi na? or Aba pi na? the other mentions the person or persons not yet come.

ba namand*h*la okuzigabisa ngokuti a ku *h*latshwe inkomo etile ezinkomeni zikayise, ngokuti i bizwe itongo. Ai; nowesifazana ka namand*h*la; noma e bonisiwe, ka yi 'kutsho; noma e se gula kakulu, ka yi 'kutsho 'luto ngenkomo; kupela u gabe ngenyanga yodwa.

Ku ti ke uma se ku yiwe enyangeni, inyanga i ku tsho konke loko a ku bonayo lowo 'muntu. Uma se ku buyiwe, ba m tetise lowo 'muntu ngokuti, "Ku ngani ukuba loku ukufa wa ku bona, si ku buza kangaka, u nga ze wa si tshela na? Wa w esaba ni? Kw' enza wena ini, lo kw' enza abapansi nje na?" A ti, "Nga ngi ti, 'Yizwa ni ngenyanga.'" A ku vume loko 'kutsho kwenyanga, a ti, "O, eh; i tsho konke e nga ku bonayo."

I *h*latshwe ke inkomo. Ku tiwe lapa i nga ka *h*latshwa, a pume umninimuzi, a ngene esibayeni e pete impepo. Uma ku inkomo e isidanda, a i pulule ngempepo njalo em*h*lana, a ti, "Yeti, nina 'basekutini," (lelo 'zwi lokuti yeti, izwi leli lokuti abantu a ba lalele loko oku za 'utshiwo ngaleso 'sikuleko e ku kulekwa ngaso ematongweni;

take upon themselves to say, "Let such and such a bullock among the cattle of my father be killed, for the Itongo has demanded it." No; neither can a woman; even though the Itongo has made it most evident to her, she will not say any thing about it; even though she is very ill, she will not say any thing about a bullock; she trusts only to the diviner.

When they have gone to the diviner, he will tell them every thing which the man has seen. When they come back again, they scold the man, saying, "Why, when you knew the disease, and we asked you so much, did you not tell us? What were you afraid of? Did you make yourself ill? was it not the Amatongo only?" He replies, "I said, 'Hear the diviner.'" And he assents to what the diviner has said, saying, "Yes, yes; he says all that I saw."

And so the bullock is killed. Before it is killed, the head of the village goes into the cattle-pen, carrying incense in his hand. If the bullock is tame, he gently rubs it again and again with incense on the back, and says, "All hail, Spirits of our tribe" (the word "All hail" tells all the people to listen to what is about to be said in the prayer which is made to the

nembala ke ku tule, ku ti nya ekaya, ku nga bi ko umsindo wokukuluma; ku kulume yena lowo 'muntu yedwa; abantu be lalele, e kuluma namadhlozi, e ti,) "Kuhle ini, abantu be njengani nje, ukuba ni zinge ni ti lapa nga ni kcela ukudhla; kepa ni zinge ni fika ngokufa ngezikati zonke na? Kuhle loku na? Ai! A ni boni ke namhla ni hlazekile, ni nukiwe inyanga? Loku ku fanele ukuba uma ni biza ukudhla, a ngi yi 'kunqaba. Nako ke ukudhla kwenu. Bízana ni nonke nina 'bakwiti. A ngi zi 'kutsho ukuti, 'Bani, nank' ukudhla kwako,' ngokuba ni nomona. Kodwa wena, 'bani, o gulisa lo 'muntu, mema bonke, ni ze 'kudhla loku 'kudhla. Uma ku uwena ngi za 'ubona pela ngalo 'muntu e ku tiwa u patwe uwe. A ng' azi ke loko e u ku bizayo. Se ngi ku nikile. Ka sinde lo 'muntu. Ni hlangane nonke, nina 'basekutini, e na ti na ti" (e tsho e ba weza ngamazibuko e bala ubukqawe babo uma be sa hamba).

Amatongo; and truly they are silent—not a sound is heard, nor the least talking; the chief man only speaks, and the people listen whilst he is speaking to the Amatongo, saying) "Is it proper that people like you should habitually, instead of asking for food in a proper manner,—should habitually come to us at all times in the form of sickness? Is that proper? No! Do you not then see that you are disgraced this day, having been smelt out by the diviner? For it is proper if you demand food, that I should not refuse it. There then is your food. All ye spirits of our tribe, summon one another. I am not going to say, 'So-and-so, there is thy food,' for you are jealous.[36] But thou, So-and-so, who art making this man ill, call all the spirits; come all of you to eat this food. If it is you I shall then see by the recovery of this man whom, it is said, you have made ill. I now no longer know what you can demand. I have already given you what you ask. Let the man get well. Come together all of you of such-and-such a people, which did so-and-so and so-and-so" (that is, he lauds them by recounting the mighty actions which they did whilst living). He is very earnest,

[36] So other heathens represent their gods as jealous. The Iliad is but a history of the results of the jealousy of two goddesses.

A tukutele ngokuti, "Se ngi ya mangala nawe, 'bani, o te wa ti, u se u zinge u fikisa kwesela; lapa u sa hamba kwa ku nge njalo; wa u kw enza konke obala. A ku pele uku ngi nyenyela. Hamba ni obala, ngi ni bone; loko e ni ku bizayo a ngi yi 'kun*q*aba nako; ngokuba nga ku piwa ini konke—izinkomo nabantwana namabele. Nesalukazi sakiti ni si bize, si ze 'kud*h*la; nengane eya fayo, a i ze 'kud*h*la; si jabule."

saying, "I now greatly wonder that you too, So-and-so, who used to do such-and-such mighty things, now continually come as a thief; whilst you were still living it was not so; you used to do every thing openly. Let this coming to me stealthily be at an end. Go openly, that I may see you, for that which you ask for I will not refuse; for you gave it all to me, —the cattle, the children, and the corn. And thou, old woman[37] of our tribe, we call you to come and eat; and the infant which is dead, let it come and eat; that we may rejoice."

Nako ke ukubonga kwabantu, be bonga id*h*lozi; i *h*latshwe ke.

Such, then, is the worship with which they worship the Itongo; and so the bullock is killed.

Ba ba *h*langanisa ngoku ba biza, ngokuba abanye a ba sa b' azi amagama abo; kepa bona aba ngapansi ba ya b' azi bonke, ba sa ba siza, a ba ba yeki; kepa ngaloko aba ngapezulu ba ti, "Woza ni nonke, ni zokud*h*la." Ngokuba kuk*q*ala kwa ku bizwa abantu ab' aziwayo; kepa ngaloko 'kwenza kwa bangwa ukufa, kwa ba kukulu; ku yiwe enyangeni ukuti,

They unite all the Amatongo in one invitation, for some of them they no longer know by name; but the dead know all of the living, and continually help them and do not forsake them; and on that account the living say, "Come, all of you, and eat." For at first those who were known were called by name; but by doing so they summoned disease, and it was very great; and they went to the diviner, saying, "Hau! what

[37] The old woman and the infant are mentioned in conclusion because he wishes to include all. The old woman and the infant are not regarded in the affairs of the village, but when they have become members of the spirit-world they are important and must be propitiated. The Itongo of an old woman is supposed to be malicious and spiteful; that of the infant is pure and beneficent. The diviner is supposed to divine by the Amatongo of infants.

"Hau! ini pela, loku si *h*labe lukulu[38] lungaka lwetu inkabi, si nga toli isikala sokupefumula na? Se ku ini?" Kepa inyanga i tsho, umuntu o nga patwanga aba nga m aziyo, isalukazi noma ingane; labo aba solayo. Kwa vela ke ukungaketi; se ku *h*langaniswa bonke.

Nako ke ukubonga kwabantu, be bonga id*h*lozi; i *h*latshwe ke. Ku ti uma a i gwaze omunye, i kale i ti be, a be e se pinda ukubonga, e ti, "Kala, nkomo yakwetu, ngokuba kwa ti, kwa ti," e balisa amatongo akubo. I we.

Ku ti uma i *h*lin*h*lwe, i botshoswe, ku be se ku tatwa um*h*lwe*h*lwe kancinyane nodengezi nela*h*le lomlilo nempepo, se ku yiwa end*h*lini lapa ku gulwayo kona; noma end*h*lini enkulu, lapa ku tiwa amatongo a *h*lala kona; ngokuba pela ku njalo, ku tiwa itongo li *h*lala end*h*lini enkulu. Ku

"What is the meaning then of this, that we have killed so great an ox of our tribe, and yet cannot get any breathing time? What is the meaning of this?" And the diviner tells them, there is a man whom they have not worshipped, whom they do not know, an old woman or an infant; it is they who find fault. And thus arose the custom of making no distinction; and all are now invited together.

Such then is the manner in which people worship the Amatongo; and then the bullock is killed. And if when another appointed for the purpose stabs it, the bullock cries,[39] the head of the village again worships, saying, "Cry, bullock of our people," and he then recounts the valorous deeds of the dead, mentioning the names of the Amatongo of their tribe. The bullock drops.

When it is skinned, it is laid open and a small piece of the caul is taken and a sherd, and a live coal, and incense, and they go with it into the house of the sick man; or into the chief house of the village where it is said the Amatongo dwell; for it is said that the Itongo lives in the great house. And the smoke arises in

[38] That is, *uluto*, something.

[39] If the bullock cries it is considered a good omen, and the man is expected to get well. But if it makes no noise they doubt whether the sacrifice is accepted and expect death.

tunyiswe ke, ku be se ku nuka ulwasu end*h*lini.

Inyongo i se i telwa ulowo 'muntu o gulayo. U ya i tela, u ya teta. (A ngi tsho ukutukutela; ukuteta ngesinye isikati ku tshiwo ukubonga.) Ku telwe ke abantu bonke balo 'muzi; abanye ba i tela ezinyaweni, abanye ba i tele ekanda, abanye ba i puze.

Ku njalo ke indaba yamad*h*lozi. Ku ti umswani u falaka*h*lwe ezind*h*lini zonke, ukuze ba d*h*le. Ku be se ku ukupela ke. Se ku d*h*liwa inyama.

Se ku bhekwa ukusinda kulo 'muntu. Uma e nga sindi, ku ya 'ku*h*latshwa enye, a ze a zi k*q*ede lowo 'muntu. Kanti u nesinye isifo. Kepa noma ku njalo, ku kona isiminya esi tolwayo emad*h*lozini; ngokuba abamnyama ba k*q*inisile ukuti, a kona, a ya ba siza. Ngokuba ukutsho kwabo ukuti a ya ba siza, a ba tsho ngamazwi ezinyanga zabo a ba bulayo kuzo; ba tsho a ba ku bona. Noma be lele ku fike umuntu owa fayo, a kulume nomuntu, a ti, "Bani, kulo 'muzi ku*h*le ku be ukuti nokuti," e tsho indaba e za

the house, and there is the odour of the burnt caul.

Then the sick man pours the gall on his body. He pours it on himself, and talks. (I do not mean he is angry, for sometimes ukuteta means to return thanks.) And all the people of the village have the gall poured on them; some pour it on their feet, some on their heads, others drink it.

Such then is the account of the Amatongo. The contents of the bullock's stomach are sprinkled in all the houses, that the Amatongo may eat. And that is the end of it; and then the flesh is eaten.

After that they look for the recovery of the man. If he does not get well, another bullock will be killed, until he kills all he has. And forsooth he has some other disease not occasioned by the Amatongo. But notwithstanding, sometimes what is said about the Amadhlozi turns out to be true; for black men steadily affirm that the Amatongo exist and help them. For when they say that the Amatongo help them, they do not say so from what diviners have said, but from what they have themselves seen. For instance, when they are asleep, a dead man appears, and talks with one of them, and says, "So-and-so, it is well that such and such be done in this village," telling him

'uvela. Njengaloku ku be ku tiwa kwabamnyama, "A ku gaywe utshwala obukulu;" nembala bu gaywe, ku tiwe, "Ku tsho id*h*lozi, li ti, 'Ngi za 'ku ni pa amabele.'" Uma se be wa zuzile ngalo 'nyaka, ba ya 'ku wa bonga; futi ekupeleni kwonyaka ba wa bonge lawo 'mabele e kwa tiwa b' eza 'ku wa piwa. I loko ke oku ba fipazayo, ukuti, "Kanti ba ya kuluma nati, si kw enze loko, si pile na? Ba bize inkomo etile ngomuntu o gulayo, a pile na?"

something that will happen. For instance, black men used to be commanded to make a great deal of beer; and so they made it, and said, "The Idhlozi says, 'I will give you corn.'" If they obtain it that year they bless the Amatongo; and at the end of the year[40] they return thanks for the corn, which they were promised. It is this which blinds them, and they say, "But do they not speak with us, and we do what they tell us to do and obtain health? Do they not demand a certain bullock of a man, and he gives it and gets well?"

The mode of slaughtering a Bullock.

LAPO ku *h*latshiwe, umnininkomo u misa umuntu ukuze a bheke, kona inkomo yake i nga yi 'kwenakala; ku be i lowo o kipa isito, a si shiyele ukuze a k*q*edele emuva isikcubi a si kipe, a fake kweyake imbiza. Ku ti kwabakipa izito, u lowo njalo o kipa isito a si shiyele ukuze ngemva a zi kipele izikcubi, a zi fake embizeni. Labo abakipayo izito ku ya bizwa kakulu kubo inyama aba seziko; ba ya

WHEN an ox is slaughtered, the owner of it appoints some one to watch lest it should be spoilt; and each one who cuts off a leg leaves a portion of it behind, that he may afterwards take the piece of flesh thus left, and put it in his own pot. For among those who separate the legs from the carcase, each one leaves portions still attached to the carcase, that he may afterwards cut them off and put them in his own pot. Those who are sitting round the fire ask for meat of those especially who cut off the legs; as they cut them

[40] That is, at the end of harvest.

kipa, ba ya ponsa njalo izikcubana, ba ya d*h*la, ba ya kala, be kala nemitama emlonyeni, be ti, "Sa tsha." U lowo njalo u pete umkonto wake, u d*h*lela pezulu, i ze i botshoswe ngapakati.

Loku ku njalonjalo kwo*h*linzayo, u lowo u pete imbiza yake, ukuze a ke ububende. Ku ti uma i tiwe k*q*eke, ku vele ububende, ku be se ku suka umuntu a be munye, o za 'ukelela ezimbizeni zonke, a zing' e ka ngendebe, e tela kuleyo na kuleyo, be zinge be dedelana, zi ze zi gcwale izimbiza. Ku ti ku be kona amagugu oku*h*linza; a buye imbiza yake i gcwele, inyama e i *h*lome na ngezinti e nga ngenanga embizeni. A fike end*h*lini yake, abantwana bake ba i d*h*le, i ba dake njengaloko kungati ku *h*labe yena.

I tutwe ke, i siwe end*h*lini, i bekelelwe emsamo 'ndawo nye; i nga pekwa ngalelo 'langa; ku d*h*liwe ububende ngalelo 'langa; ku ti ku sa i be i *h*la*h*lelwa, se i za 'upekwa; ku kitshwa nemilenze, nemi*h*lubulo noma insonyama; ku

off they throw continually small pieces of flesh to them, and they shout even with their mouths full, "We are burnt."[41] And each one has his assagai and eats standing, until the bullock is opened.

And each one that skins the bullock has his own pot, that he may pour the blood into it. When the carcase is completely opened, one arises to dip out the blood into all the pots; he dips it out with a cup and pours it into each vessel, the people giving way for each other until all the pots are full. The person who skins the bullock has the power of purloining; and he goes home with his pot full; and meat too stuck on rods which is not put into the pots. He enters his house, and his children eat, and it more than suffices them, just as though he had himself killed an ox of his own.

The meat is carried into the house and placed at the upper end in one place; it is not cooked on the day it is killed, but the blood is eaten; on the following morning it is cut up when it is going to be cooked; they separate the legs and the ribs,[42] and the

---

41 *We are scorched or burnt.*—Meaning by this they are standing before a fire with nothing between them and the flame. They wish for meat to put on the fire.

42 The *umthlubulo* is that portion of the ribs which is left after cutting away the breast or brisket, and includes the flesh down to the hip. The flesh of the flank which forms a part of the *umthlubulo* is called *itebe*.

*h*lin*h*liswa ab' elama' nayo. Ngokuba ku njalo kubantu abamnyama: omkulu w etulelwa insonyama; o ngapansi a *h*lin*h*liswe um*h*lubulo, noma umkono; umlenze u nikwe induna.

Ku ti uma i vutwe, lokupela i d*h*liwa lapa ilanga li k*q*ala ukupenduka, loku ku njalonjalo ku kandene kulowo 'muzi abantu bemizi yonke yaleso 'sizwe abaseduze, nakwamanye amaband*h*la 'akelene nalabo 'bantu. Ku ti uma se i za 'kwepulwa, bonke abantu ba ye esibayeni ngapakati, lokupela inkomo kubantu abamnyama a i d*h*lelwa end*h*lini, i d*h*lelwa kona esibayeni njalo, ukuze ku bonakale nod*h*layo nongad*h*liyo. A y epule ke ngezitebe ngezitebe, i tutwe i ngeniswe esibayeni, i bekwe 'ndawo nye ukuba y abiwe; a y a*h*lukanise njengokuma kwamaband*h*la; izinsizwa zi be nesitebe sazo, namake*h*la namadoda amakulu; kw abelwe nabezizwe. Ku ti uma ku kona noma emunye o vela kwamanye amaband*h*la o nge si ye walapo, isitebe sake si be sodwa, ku tiwe, "Nansi yasekutini." A bonge naye, a tate abantu balapo ukuze a d*h*le nabo.

insonyama;[43] and give to those who are of their house. For this is the custom with black men: the insonyama is taken to the eldest; the ribs are given to the next, or the shoulder; and the leg is given to the officer.

When the meat is cooked, for it is eaten when the sun is declining, men belonging to all the villages of the tribe, and strangers who are neighbours, press together to the village. When the meat is about to be taken from the pots, all the people go into the cattle-pen, for among black men cattle are not eaten indoors, but always in the cattle-pen, that those who are eating, and those who are not, may be seen. The chief of the village takes out the meat and puts it on the various feeding-mats, and it is carried into the cattle-pen, and put in one place, that it may be distributed; he distributes it in accordance with the positions of the assembly; the young men have their mats; those with head-rings, and the chief men, have theirs; and strangers have theirs. And if there be only one who belongs to another people, his feeding-mat is by itself, and they say to him, "Here is the meat of such a place." He thanks them, and takes people belonging to the place that he may eat with them.

---

43 The *insonyama* is the superficial layer of flesh from the hip to the ear, including the pectoral muscles.

Ku ti uma ba d*h*le bonke, abanye ba k*q*ede kuk*q*ala, b' esuke kwesabo isitebe, b' elekela aba sa d*h*lako, ba ti, "O, a si n' elekele; si ya bona ukuba ni ya *h*lupeka."

Ku ti uma i pele i ti du, ba nga k*q*ali ba valelise; ku landwe um*h*luzi, nobubende obu buya bu pume emva kwenyama, obu salako.

Ku ti uma ku pele konke loku, 'esuke umnimuzana, nomunye umuntu o pete isitebe, 'enyuke kancane, a ti, "Tula ni, ni ti nya." Nembala ku ti nya. A ti, "Ehe; nina 'bakwiti, e na ti na ti, ngi ya kuleka, ngi kuleka ubu*h*le ngemva kwale 'nkomo yakwetu. Ngi ti, ku nge ti, lokupela izinkomo lezi zi kona nje, ngi zi piwa inina. Kepa uma ni biza ukud*h*la kumina e ni ngi pa kona, a ku fanele ini ukuba ngi ni pe kona na? Ngi kuleka izinkomo, ukuba zi gcwale kulesi 'sibaya. Ngi kulekela amabele, ku ngene abantu abaningi kulo 'muzi wenu, ba kxokozele, ba dumise nina. Ngi kcela nenzalo, ukuba lo 'muzi u kcume, ukuze igama lenu li nga peli." A k*q*ede ke.

When all have eaten, and some have finished before the rest, they join themselves with those who are still eating, and say, "O, let us join with you; we see you are in trouble."

When it is all eaten they do not begin to take leave; but the broth, and the blood which is still uneaten, are brought out after the meat.

When all is finished, the head man and another man who carries a feeding-mat go a little towards the head of the cattle-pen, and the head man says, "Be perfectly silent." And the assembly becomes very silent. He says, "Yes, yes; our people, who did such and such noble acts, I pray to you—I pray for prosperity, after having sacrificed this bullock of yours. I say, I cannot refuse to give you food, for these cattle which are here you gave me. And if you ask food of me which you have given me, is it not proper that I should give it to you? I pray for cattle, that they may fill this pen. I pray for corn, that many people may come to this village of yours, and make a noise, and glorify you. I ask also for children, that this village may have a large population, and that your name may never come to an end." So he finishes.

Ba valelise ke bonke basemizini, ba pume, ba goduke. Lokupela uma ku inala kw enziwe notshwala obukulu. Ku ti eyamanina inyama i be yodwa; ku ya *h*lakazeka amabandh*l*a e ti nya, ku *h*langana amanina, 'epula eyawo. Nemizi e seduze i bizane ukuza 'kud*h*la inyama kulowo 'muzi. I pele ke. Ba goduke bonke.

So all strangers take leave, and go home. And if it is a time of plenty, much beer is also made. And the meat of the women is by itself; when the men have departed and the place is still, the women come together and take out their meat. And neighbouring villages send messages one to another to come and eat meat at the village. So it is all eaten, and they go home.

Laying the Spirit of Divination.

INDABA ngokuvinjwa kwomuntu o netongo lokubula, uma e ng' azi ukuba u pupa amapupa a k*q*onde pi; u zinge e pupa njalo izinyoka eziningi zi m tandela umzimba wonke e semanzini, e sesizibeni; u ya puma u se sindwa izinyoka: e wela nomfula u gcwele. U ze umzimba wake w enyele, e ng' azi ukuba lawo 'mapupa emi*h*la yonke a komba ni na.

THE account of barring the way against a spirit of divination which visits a man when he does not understand the meaning of his dreams; he dreams continually of many snakes encircling his whole body whilst he is in a pool of water; he quits the water heavy with snakes: or he dreams he is crossing a flooded river. At length his body is relaxed, he not knowing what is the meaning of those daily dreams.

A ze a gule; ku be kona nokud*h*la a ziliswa kona, e tshelwa e lele, ukuti, "Ukud*h*la okutile u nga ku d*h*li." Nembala a ku yeke. Uma e ku d*h*la ngenkani, umzimba u nga tokozi. A ze a ku yeke ngokuti, "Ngi petwe."

At length he becomes ill; and there is certain food he is obliged to abstain from, being told in his sleep not to eat such and such food. So he no longer eats that food. If he eat it from opposition, his health suffers. At length he leaves it alone, saying, "A spirit has visited me."

Uma e tanda ukuba inyanga, a ye enyangeni yokubula; i m pe*h*lele ubulawo obum*h*lope, i m kcakcambise, ukuze amapupa a kanye, a nga bi lufifi.

If he wishes to be a diviner, he goes to a diviner; the diviner prepares for him white ubulawo,[44] and makes him white, that his dreams may be clear, and no longer uncertain.

Uma e nga tandi, nabakubo be nga tandi, ku funwe imvu yoku m vimba, nenyanga e nge si yo yokubula, inyanga enkulu yoku m vimba. Ku ti ngam*h*la e pupile kakulu amatongo, e m twesa ubunyanga, i bizwe inyanga, i ze nemiti emnyama, ku *h*latshwe imvu, ku tatwe umswani wayo, ku kandwe imiti emnyama, a puziswe; a *h*lanzele esitsheni, ku fakwe umswani wemvu; ku yiswe loko emhumeni o nga neti nakanye, ku mbelwe pansi, ku vinjwe ngom*h*laba; umuntu a nga bheki ngemuva a z' a fike 'kaya, e nga bhekanga emuva. I loko ke ukuvinjwa kwetongo. Ku ti noma li fika kuye ngobusuku, li nga be li sa kanya, ku be mnyama, a nga be e

If he does not wish to be a diviner, nor his friends, they take a sheep for the purpose of barring the way of the spirit, and a doctor who is not a diviner is consulted —a doctor of celebrity—for the purpose of barring the way. When he has dreamed a great deal of the spirits, and they initiate him into the knowledge proper to doctors, the doctor is called, and comes with black medicines;[45] a sheep is killed, and the contents of the paunch are taken, and the black medicines bruised, and the man is made to drink them; he throws the contents of his stomach into a vessel, and the contents of the sheep's stomach are added to them; this is taken to a cave into which no rain enters; it is buried there in the earth, and closed up with soil; and the doctor does not look behind him till he gets home. This, then, is the method of barring the way against a spirit. And though it come to him by night, it is no longer distinctly visible, but obscure, and the man

[44] See Note above, p. 142.

[45] Black medicines, that is, medicines which have the power of rendering the Itongo dark or indistinct.

sa bonisisa ka*h*le njengokuk*q*ala, li muke ke, a zi d*h*le zonke izid*h*lo, a nga zili 'luto.

Kepa kwabanye u vinjwa, ku ye ngako; kwabanye a ku yi ngako; ku y' a*h*luleka, lo 'muntu a fe ngokubangwa amatongo nabahambayo; a fe masinyane. I loko ke e ngi ku zwayo.

no longer sees it distinctly as at first; and so it departs, and he eats all kinds of food, and abstains from nothing.

And with some the way is barred successfully; with others without success; it is tried to no purpose, and the man dies through being claimed at the same time by the Amatongo and by living men, and dies very soon. This, then, is what I have heard.

The subject of the following narrative was a convert of some eleven or twelve years' standing. He has always manifested great uncertainty of character and a very impressible nervous system, and for many years has had from time to time subjective apparitions, and been in the habit of dreaming strange, life-like dreams. One day he suddenly left the mission station. The following account was obtained from a native who was sent to enquire of him at the village where he was living. I have had an opportunity of seeing him since the underneath was given me. He has many symptoms of hysteria, appears fully to believe in his feelings; and yet at the same time to be practising deceit on others, and probably too on himself.

Indaba yokugula kukajames, u gula ukufa oku nga k*q*ondeki kubantu aba amakolwa; ngokuba ku ti noma umuntu ku nga u y' etasa, ku ti a nga ya eskoleni, ku pele loko ngokuzing' ezwa izwi lenkosi. Baningi aba be njalo, se kwa pela. Kepa ngaye umuntu omdala kangaka, ku ya mangalisa ukuba a

The account of the illness of James, which is not intelligible among Christians; for although a person may appear to be affected with those symptoms which precede the power of divination, yet when he goes to a mission station all that ceases through continually hearing the word of God. There are many who were so affected, but are now so no longer. But as regards him who is now so old, it is marvellous

k*q*alwe ile 'nto njengokungati u ya fika emzini wamakolwa.

Nga fika si nopaulu, si hamba ngoku m zuma ukuti, "Ka nga si zwa, ka nga si boni; ka k*q*abuke si ngena nje end*hl*ini e nga ka zilungisi, si bone ukuma kwake uma e nga boni 'muntu ukuba u se njani na."

Sa fika e lele, 'embete izingubo ezimbili—enye imnyama, enye impofu, se i guga. Wa si bona, wa lala, wa tula. Nga m vusa, nga ti, "Vuka." Wa zibinya, e ti, "Ake w enze ka*hl*e; ngi za 'uvuka. Ngi pangise ni! Ngi pangise ni! Kw enze njani ekaya na?" Kwa za kwa ba isikati e nga vuki.

Wa vuka ke, wa si bingelela. Sa vuma. Nga m buza ukuti, "U njani, james, na?" Wa ti, "Ngi ya gula kakulu." Nga ti, "U nani na?" Wa ti, "Ngi nokufa e ngi nga kw azi." Nga ti, "Ngi landise konke." Wa k*q*ala ngokuti:

"O, nembala, u k*q*inisile. Uma ku buza umfana nje, ngi be ngi nga yi 'kutsho 'luto nakanye.

that he should begin to be so affected, as though he had only just come to a Christian village.

I and Paul reached the place where he is, going with the intention of taking him by surprise, saying to each other, "Do not let him hear or see us; let him first see us when we are already in the hut, before he puts himself to rights, that we may see what he does now when no man is looking at him."

When we came he was lying down covered with two blankets—one black, the other grey and old. When he saw us he remained lying and was silent. I aroused him, saying, "Arouse." He writhed himself and said, "Just have patience. I am about to arise. Make haste and tell me! Make haste and tell me! What has happened at home?" But it was a long time before he arose.

At length he arose and saluted us; and we saluted him. I asked him, saying, "James, how are you?" He said, "I am very ill." I said, "What is the matter with you?" He said, "I have a disease with which I am not acquainted." I said, "Tell me all about it." He began by saying:

"O, truly, you are right. If it were a mere boy who asked, I would not say a single word. But

Kepa lok' u buza wena, a ngi zi 'kushiya 'luto. Kukqala nga ng' esaba, ngi ti, 'Ku za 'utiwa ni?' Kepa namhla loku loku 'kufa se ku ng' ahlukanisile nani, ngi nge fihle 'luto.

"Kade loku 'kufa kwa ngi kqala, ngi nga ka pumi na sekaya lapaya, ukubuyela endhlini le entsha yami; kwa ngi kqala ngi se pakati kwomuzi. Nabakamapontshi laba ba ya kw azi. Kepa kwa buya kwa pela. Ukwenza kwako kukqala ngokukupuka eminweni na semizwanini, ku kupuke ngemikono na ngemilenze; ku gijima ku ti saka nomzimba wonke; kw enyuke, ku ze pezulu nomzimba, ku fike ku me emahlombe, kw enze umsiti ku be nzima kakulu lapa; ku nga ti ngi twele into e sindayo.

"Kepa manje a ku se loko kodwa; ngokuba manje se zi kona izinto e ngi zi bonayo ngesikati sokulala. Ekupumeni kwami ekaya, ngi pume se ngi kqambe amagama amatatu, ngi nga w' azi ukuba a vela pi na; ngi zwe igama, se ngi li hlabelele nje, ngi li kqede lonke, ngi nga li fundanga.

"Kepa into e ngi hlupa kakulu manje, ukuba izwe leli lonke a ku ko e ngi nga l' aziyo; ngi li kqeda

since it is you who ask, I will tell you everything. At first I was afraid, and said, 'What will men say?' But now since this disease has separated me from you, I can make no concealment.

"Long ago this disease began, even before I quitted the house on the other side of the river to go to my new house; it began whilst I still lived in the village. And the family of Umapontshi know it. But it passed off again. It first began by creeping up from my fingers and toes; it then crept up my arms and thighs; it ran and spread itself over the whole body, until it reached the upper part of the body, and stopped in my shoulders, and caused a sensation of oppression, and there was a great weight here on my shoulders; it was as if I was carrying a heavy weight.

"But now it is not that only; but now there are things which I see when I lie down. When I left home I had composed three songs, without knowing whence they came; I heard the song, and then just sang it, and sang the whole of it without having ever learnt it.

"But that which troubles me most now is, that there is not a single place in the whole country which I do not know; I go over

lonke ebusuku ngi lele; a ng' azi lapa ngi ng' aziyo uma u pi na.

"Ngi bona nezind*h*lovu nezimpisi, nezingonyama nezingwe nezinyoka, nemifula i gcwala. Konke loku ku *h*langana kumi, ku za 'u ngi bulala. Amasuku onke, a ku ko 'langa ngi ke ngi lale ngi nga bonanga.

"Futi, ngi bone se ngi ndiza, ngi nga sa nyateli pansi lapa."

Nga buza ukuti, "Loku se ku njalo, inkosi yako u sa i kumbula njena na?"

Wa ti, "K*q*a. Se ku ukufa loko. Uma ngi linga ukuti, 'A ngi tandaze,' ku nga ti ngi biza ukufa konke ukuba ku ngi bulale masinyane. Iudaba yenkosi se i kitshiwe kumi ilesi 'sifo. Se ku fulatele sona kupela."

Nga ti, "U ya kumbula indaba yepupa elidala lako na?"

Wa ti, "U tsho lemikumbu na?"

Nga ti, "Yebo."

Wa ti, "Au! A ngi ko*h*lwa

it all by night in my sleep; there is not a single place the exact situation of which I do not know.

"I see also elephants and hyenas, and lions, and leopards, and snakes, and full rivers. All these things come near to me to kill me. Not a single day passes without my seeing such things in my sleep.

"Again, I see that I am flying, no longer treading on this earth."

I asked him, "Since it is thus with you, do you still remember your Lord?"

He said, "No. To do so is death to me. If I try, saying, 'Let me pray,' it is as if I summoned all kinds of death to come and kill me at once. The Lord's tidings are plucked out of me by this disease. It alone has now the dominion over me."

I said, "Do you remember that old dream[46] of yours?"

He said, "Do you speak of that of the boats?"

I said, "Yes."

He replied, "Oh! I do not

---

[46] This dream was recorded at the time. He dreamt that he was crossing a river with Umpengula in a boat. When they were in the middle of the river, without any apparent cause, the bottom of the boat opened and let him through, and, after struggling for a time in the water, he found himself on a sandbank in the midst of the stream, and saw Umpengula on the other side, he having reached without difficulty the place of their destination. All this time he seemed to himself as one dead, though not deprived of sensation—that is, he thought he had died. He found himself surrounded by huge dogs, which appeared ready to devour him, and many black people, among whom he observed his own mother, who expressed her wonder at finding him among them.—This is just one of those prophetic dreams

ilo. Ngi li bona ka*hl*e nam*hl*a nje ukuba umkumbu 'lukolo lwami o se lu tshonile namu*hl*a. Nezinja lezo e nga zi bona zi ya ngi d*hl*a nam*hl*a nje."

Nga ti, "Kepa uma inkosi yako se isita kuwe, u ya 'kusinda ngobani na?"

Wa ti, "K*q*a. Se ngi file kupela. A ngi tsho ukuba ngi sa 'uba umuntu wokuba ku ngene ukuma okutsha e ngi nga ku k*q*ondi nakanye. A ng' azi ukuba ngi ini. Bheka, ngokuba ngi umuntu o tanda abantwana bami kakulu. Kepa nam*hl*a nje a ngi sa b' azi noma ba kona ini. Into enkulu i lesi 'sifo kupela."

Wa ti, "Manje se ngi ke ngi pume ebusuku, ngi yalelwe umuti, ku tiwe, u sendaweni etile; a ngi ye 'ku u mba. Ngi pume, ngi fike kona, ngi nga u boni, ngi zule nje, ngi ze ngi buye. Se ku njalo manje kumi.

forget it. I see clearly now that the boat is my faith, which has now sunk into the water. And the dogs which I saw are now devouring me."

I said, "But if your Lord is now your enemy, who will save you?"

He replied, "No. I am now dead altogether. I do not think that I am still a man who can enter into a new position, which I do not in the least understand.[47] I do not know what I am. Attend, for I am a man who loves my children dearly. But now I do not care whether they are alive or not. The great thing is this disease alone."

He continued, "And now I begin to go out by night, having an internal intimation about medicine;[48] it is said, 'The medicine is in such a place; go and dig it up.' I go out and reach the place, but do not find the medicine;[49] I merely walk up and down, and at length return. This is my present state.

---

which is suggested to a man by his own thoughts and wishes, and which help on its own fulfilment by placing before his mind during sleep a distinct tableau of the future such as whilst awake he would be afraid to form for himself.

47 That is, he no longer understands the Christian faith, and does not believe it can again enter him; or that he can change again.

48 Lit., Having had a charge given me respecting a medicine, or plant possessed of medical properties. The charge, of course, being supposed to be given by the Itongo.

49 It is said to be thus with those who are about to be diviners; they are often deceived before they learn to comprehend the voices of the Itongo by which they are called.

"Ziningi iziuto e ku nga ti ngi ya zi bona, ngi fike kona ngi nga zi boni. Ku ze kwa ti ngolunye usuku ekuseni kakulu, kwa tiwa, a ngi ye 'kumba umuti. Nga hamba, nga fika kona, a nga u bona; nga buya. Ngi te ngi fika ekaya, kwa ku tiwa, 'U shiyele ni umuti na? i wona lowo o ke wa u bona. Hamba, u ye 'ku u mba.' Nga za nga hamba, nga fika nga u mba. Nga buya nga u la*h*la, ngokuba ngi ng' azi ukuba ngi za 'kwenza ni ngawo. Omunye kwa tiwa, a ngi ye 'ku u mba esi*h*lutankungu. Ng' ala; na nam*h*la nje a ngi yanga.

"There are many things which I seem to see, but when I go to them I cannot see them. At length it happened one day very early in the morning, I was told to go and dig up some medicine. I went to the place, but did not see the medicine, and came back again. When I reached home, it was said, 'Why have you left the medicine? it is that which you saw. Go and dig it up.' At length I went to the place and dug it up. Again I threw it away, for I did not know what to do with it. I was told to go and dig up another medicine on the Isithlutankungu. I refused, and I have not been to this day.

"Kepa into enkulu inyama; ku tiwa njalonjalo, 'A ku *h*latshwe.' Ku nga ti ngi nga d*h*la inyama imi*h*la yonke. Ku funa inyama loku 'kufa; kepa a ngi vumi.

"But the great thing is meat; it is said constantly, 'Let a bullock be killed.'[50] It is as though I could eat meat daily. This disease longs for meat; but I will not kill cattle.

"Ngi *h*lutshwa izinja; ku nga ti lapa ngi kona inja i nge tshaywe; ngi y' esaba kakulu. Nenyanga yokubula ku nga ti ngi nge i bone; ku nga fika yona, ngi ya fa masinyane, ngi we pansi, ngi fe. I loko ke oku ngi *h*lupayo. Manje a ngi sa tandi 'muntu. In*h*liziyo yami a i sa ba tandi aba-

"I am harassed by the dogs; it is as if where I am the dogs must not be beaten; I am greatly afraid of the noise. And it is as though I could not look on a diviner; he may come, I am at once in a dying state, and fall down and die. It is this, then, that troubles me. And now I no longer love any one. My heart no longer loves

[50] Not that he likes meat; he eats only a small quantity; but it is the custom with such people to ask to have sacrifices continually made to the Amatongo. It is therefore common when these symptoms first manifest themselves to seek means for laying the Itongo, lest the frequent sacrifices demanded should impoverish them.

ntu. Ku nga ti ngi nga *h*lala lapa ku te nya, ku ng' ezwakali umsindo nakanye. A ng' azi uma u ti a ngi buye nje, ngi ya 'ku*h*lala pi, loku insimbi kwiti i kala futifuti. A ngi *h*langani nomsindo onjalo; ngi y' esaba kakulu. A ngi yi 'ku*h*lala. Ngi ya 'kukitshwa insimbi."

Kwa ba njalo ke sa kuluma ngokubuya, ngi ti, "Buya, uma u gulela lapa, umkako e nga ku boni, ka taho ukuba u y' elatshwa nakanye. Kuyena u m shiyile nje, ukuba ku ya 'kuti um*h*la ku fike uyise a m tate, a hambe naye. U y' azi nawe ukuba abafazi betu ba ya kuluma, noma ku nga guli 'muntu, ba si tshele ukuti, 'Uma indoda i *h*lubuka, i buyela ngapand*h*le, i donswa ubumnandi bakona, kona mina, ngokuba a ngi b' azi ubumnandi bakona, se ng' a*h*lukana nayo masinyane, ngi nge fe ngokufa komunye umuntu e zibulala ngamabomu.' A ngi ti u y' azi ukuba ba taho njalo abafazi betu na?"

Wa vuma, wa ti, "Yebo. Uhannah u fikile lapa ngensuku ezi d*h*lulile. Wa ti, a ngi kipe loku 'kufa; uma ku nga pumi, si ya 'kwa*h*lukana. Nga m pendula ngokuti, 'Ukukipa ukufa ukwenza

men. It is as though I could stay where it is perfectly still—where there is not the least sound. When you tell me to return, I do not know where I could stay, for the bell of our village sounds again and again. I do not like such a sound as that; I am much afraid. I shall not stay. I shall be driven away by the bell."

And then we spoke of his return, I saying, "Come home, if you are ill here; your wife, not seeing you, does not suppose at all that you are under medical treatment. To her way of thinking, you have merely forsaken her; therefore when her father comes he will come and take her away with him. You know yourself that our wives talk, and although a man is not sick, they tell us that if a husband rebels and returns to heathen life, attracted by its pleasant things, yet his wife, because she does not know any pleasant things of heathen life, will at once separate from him, and not die with the death with which another wilfully kills himself. Do you not know that our wives say thus?"

He assented and said, "Yes. Hannah came here some days ago. She told me to get rid of this disease. And if I did not get rid of it, we should separate. I answered her and asked, 'What is meant

njani na? Ngi ya ku tanda ini na? Kw' enziwa imi ini na? O, a ngi kw azi ukukitshwa kwokufa. Umniniko o gula iko.' S' ahlukana ke. Nami ngi za 'kubuya ngalelo 'zwi lokuti, 'Uma ku nga pumi, si za 'kwahlukana.' Se ngi za 'ubuya, naye umkami a zibonele loko oku nga kipa loku 'kufa. Ngi nge tsho usuku. Ni ya 'ubona ngi fika nje. Umzimba wami ubuhlungu, ngokuba ngalobu 'busuku e ni fika ngabo ngi ni bonile ni za kumi, ni abelungu. Wa ngi bulala umlungu; wa ngena lapa, wa ngi tshaya emlenzeni lo ow' apukayo, wa w apula. Ng' esuka, nga m tela ngomlota. Ngi gula iloko ke. Ngi y' ahluleka uku ni tshela usuku.

by getting rid of it? Am I fond of it? Did I produce it? O, I do not know how the disease can be got rid of. The disease is master of the sick man.' And so we separated. And I am now about to return home for that saying of hers, 'If the disease does not cease we shall separate.' I will now come back, that my wife may see for herself that which can get rid of the disease. I cannot fix the day. You will see me when I come. My body is in pain, for on the night before you came I saw you coming to me, but you were white men. A white man hurt me; he came in here and struck me on the thigh which was broken, and broke it again. I arose and threw ashes over him.[51] I am ill from that then. I cannot tell you the day.

"A ngi guli imihla yonke. Ngolunye usuku ngi ya tokoza nje, kakulu ngesonto. Ku ti ngalo, noma ngi nga sa l' azi, ngi ya pila kakulu. Se ng' azi ngomzimba ukuba isonto namhla nje. Ku njalo ke ukufa kwami.

"I am not ill every day. Some days I am quite well, especially on Sunday. On Sunday, although I no longer know it is Sunday, I am very well. I now know by my body that it is Sunday. Such then is my disease.

"Hamba ni. Ke ngi ni pelezele; ngi za 'kubuya lapa ngapezulu."

"Go. I will accompany you; I will come back from the top of the hill."

Nembala ke sa hamba nje naye. Kodwa u se hamba-ze, u se binca imintsha. Nga ka nga u bona umuntsha wake, isitobo esimnyama.

So then we went with him. But he now goes naked, and wears the umuntsha. I just caught sight of his umuntsha; the hinder part was black.

[51] That is, in a dream.

Futi nga buza ngokuti, "Ku ngani ukuba u pume ekaya ngokunyenyela umfundisi, o inyanga yezifo zonke, u nga m tshelanga na?"

Wa ti, "A ngi m tshelanga ngokuba ng' esaba, nga ti, 'Uma ngi m tshela, u za 'kuti ngi ya *h*lanya, a ngi bambe, a ngi yise emgungund*h*lovu, ngi *h*lale kona isikati eside.' Ng' esaba loko ke, ngi nga m tshelanga nje ngokuti, 'O, loku u*h*lanya l' ona izinto zabantu, mina a ng' oni 'luto, ngi ya zigulela nje;—O, k*q*a, a ngi nga m tsheli. Kumbe ngi ya 'kupila uma ngi zifunele izinyanga. A ngi hambe.' Nga hamba ke. Nga hamba ngaloko ke.

Sa hamba ke, s' a*h*lukana naye en*h*la kwomuzi, e hamba e nga k*x*ugi; umlenze a w omile; u lingana nomunye nje. Kodwa ekwe*h*leni ku ya bonakala ukuba lo 'muntu wa limala. Kodwa ekwenyukeni u hambisa kwabantu nje bonke.

Ukud*h*la a ku d*h*layo kutatu kupela—inyama, izinsipo ku gaywe umk*c*uku; uma ku nge ko a d*h*le imifino yasen*h*le. Nako ukud*h*la a pila ngako. Amasi ka wa faki nakanye; u ya zondana nawo.

Further, I asked him, "Why did you leave home unknown to our Teacher, who is a doctor of all diseases, without telling him?"

He replied, "I did not tell him, for I was afraid, and said, 'If I tell him, he will say I am mad, and seize me and send me to Pietermaritzburg, and I shall stay there a long time.' I feared that then, and did not tell him, thinking, 'O, since a mad man destroys people's property, and I do no harm, but my sickness is an injury to myself only;—O, no, let me not tell him. It may be I shall get well if I find doctors for myself. Let me go.' So I went away."

So we left, and separated from him at a place above the village. He walked without limping; his thigh has not dried up, it is of the same length as the other. But when he is going down hill, it is evident that he is a man who has been injured. But when he goes up hill, he looks like all other men.

There are only three kinds of food that he eats—meat, and the dregs of beer mixed with boiled maize; if these cannot be had he eats wild herbs. That is the food on which he lives. He does not put amasi into his mouth by any means; he dislikes it, and it disagrees with him.

Futi, ngolunye usuku ebusuku wa tshelwa ukuti, "Vuka, u tshone ngalapa emfuleni, u za 'kufumana inyamazane i sem*h*lon*h*lweni i banjiwe; hamba, u ye 'ku i tata." U ti, "Nga vuka ke. Kwa ti lapa se ngi hambile umfo wetu wa ngi landela, Umankamane." Wa ponsa ngetshe, wa tshaya in*h*laba. W' etuka Ujames, wa baleka, wa buyela kuye, wa m tetisa ngokuti, "W enze ni ukuba u ng' etuse lapa ngi za 'kutata inyamazane yami na?" Kwa ku pela ke, kwa pela loko o be ku m k*q*uba ukuba a yotata inyamazane. Ba goduka nje ke, ku nga se ko 'luto.

Ku tiwa abakubo, lu*h*lobo olubutataka kakulu, lu ba izinyanga. Ku kona ababili abafo wabo bakwazulu ba izinyanga. Ujames wa ngi tshela, wa ti, "Kwa fika Uheber lapa, e vela kwazulu; wa ngi tshela ukuti, 'Abafo wenu kwazulu le se be izinyanga, Ubani nobani.'" U ti ke Ujames ke, "Nanko ke umuntu owa ngi bangela ukufa loku. Wa ti e sa tsho nje nga tshaywa uvalo olwesabekayo. A ngi m pendulanga; nga tula nje. Se ngi *h*labekile, ngokuba e kuluma indaba ey' enzekayo kumina; kodwa ngi nga kulumi ngayo, ngi ng' azi ukuba isifo sini na. Yena wa ng' azisa, ku ze ku be nam*h*la nje.

Again, once at night he was told to awake and go down to the river, and he would find an antelope caught in a Euphorbia tree; and to go and take it. "So," said he, "I awoke. When I had set out, my brother, Umankamane, followed me." He threw a stone and struck an aloe. James was frightened, and ran back to him and chided him, saying, "Why did you frighten me when I was about to lay hold on my antelope." That was the end of it, and he was not again told by any thing to go and fetch the antelope. They went home, there being nothing there.

James's people say they are of a family who are very sensitive, and become doctors. There are two of his brothers in Zululand who are doctors. James told me, saying, "Heber came to us on his arrival from Zululand; he told me that my brothers in Zululand are now doctors, So-and-so and So-and-so." And so James said, "He then is the man who brought this disease on me. Whilst he was telling me I was seized with a fearful dread. I did not answer him, but remained silent. I am now ill because he spoke of what I myself was experiencing; but I did not speak of it, for I did not know what disease it was. He made me understand; and I understand it to this day."

Ku tiwa uyise kajames, Ukokela, wa e umuntu o inceku yenkosi yakwazulu. Kepa wa banjwa iso lesi 'sifo sokwetasa. Inkosi ya tukutela uma i zwe loko. Ya mu d*h*la izinkomo zonke zake. Wa *h*lala nje. Nanko ke umuti owona w' elapa Ukokela. Kwa pela.

It is said that James's father, Ukokela, was the steward of the Zulu king. But he was seized with the disease which precedes the power to divine. The king was angry when he heard it. He ate up all his cattle. That was the medicine which cured Ukokela. That was the end of it.

Abanye ba izinyanga na lapa esilungwini. Odade wabo ba y' etasa njalo; baningi aba nalesi 'sifo esi kujames. Abanye ba ya vinjwa, ku pele. Abanye ku ze ku zipelele nje, ku katale, ku m yeke. Omunye, ka si ye wakubo, ngi mu zwile lapa kujojo; intombi yasembo kanoponya; ku tiwa naye u be tasa, 'enza njengojames njalo. Kepa w' elatshwa izinyanga eziningi. Z' a*h*luleka, e se hamba ezintabeni, e nga sa *h*lali ekaya; umfazi. Wa za w' elatshwa Ujojo kamanzezulu; wa m a*h*lula. Wa *h*laba izimbuzi ezimbili — imvu nembuzi; imbuzi im*h*lope, imvu imnyama. Wa m elapa ngazo; emnyama ey' enza ukuba itongo li be mnyama, li nga kanyi; em*h*lope ey' enza ukuba itongo li be m*h*lope, li kanye, li m bonise ka*h*le.

Others are doctors here in the country of the English. His sisters have the initiatory symptoms; there are many who have James's disease. Some have the Itongo laid. With others the disease ceases of its own accord; it is tired, and leaves them. Another, not one of James's relatives, I heard Ujojo mention her; she was a girl of the Abambo, the daughter of Unoponya; it is said, she was affected, and did as James does. But she was treated by many doctors. They could not cure her; she still went to the mountains, and did not stay at home; she was a married woman. At length she was treated by Ujojo, the son of Umanzezulu; he cured her. He killed two goats—or, rather, a sheep and a goat; the goat was white, the sheep black. He treated her with them; the black sheep made the Itongo indistinct, and no longer bright; the white goat made the Itongo white and bright, that it might make her see clear-

Wa m vimba ke, wa m godusa, wa m *hl*alis' ekaya. U se umuntu nje manje. Nami ngi ke nga m bona. Kwa tiwa, kade e hamba ezintabeni. Kepa manje ka sa bonakali ukuba u ke wa hamba.

ly.[52] So he laid the Itongo, and she went home; he caused her to live at home. And she is now a human being. It is said, for a long time she lived in the mountains. But it is now no longer apparent that she ever did so.

Izinyanga zokubula zi ti ku-james, naye u ya tasa, u za 'kuba inyanga. Kodwa ka ng' elatshwa ngemiti emnyama yoku m vimba; u ya 'kufa; ka yekwe nje. Ngaloko ke abakubo se be ko*hl*iwe into a ba za 'ku y enza, loku ku tiwa, u ya 'kufa. Se be buka nje. Izwi lezinyanga li umteto kubo; ba nge li d*hl*ule nakanye.

UMPENGULA MBANDA.

The diviners tell James that he too is beginning, and will soon be a doctor. But they say he must not be treated with black medicines to lay the Itongo, for he will die; he must be just left alone. His friends therefore do not know what to do, since it is said, he will die. They merely look on. The diviners' word is their law; they can on no account go beyond it.

How to distinguish Snakes which are Amatongo from common Snakes.

UKUPENDUKA kwabantu be penduka izinyoka, lezo 'nyoka a ba ba i zo a ziningi, zi ketiwe, zi y' aziwa, —ukuti, imamba emnyama, nenyandezulu e imamba elu*hl*aza; amakosi lawo ke. Abantu um-

THE snakes into which men turn are not many; they are distinct and well known. They are the black Imamba, and the green Imamba, which is called Inyandezulu. Chiefs turn into these.

[52] This, as it is told in the text, is not clear. It appears that the doctor pursued two systems of treatment, with opposite objects. And this was really the case. He first tried the "darkening" system, by using together with the black sheep other medicines possessed of a darkening power; but not succeeding, he tried the opposite system—the "brightening" plan, that is, he acted subtlely, making the Itongo bright and clear, and willing to come near the patient, and then by suddenly again resorting to the "darkening" system, he made the Itongo dark for ever, and so "the spirit was laid," and has never appeared since.

*hl*wazi, amakosikazi ke lawo. E-nye ubulube ukuti inkwakwa, nomzingand*hl*u, kupela kwezinyoka ezi abantu.

Kepa ukubonwa kwazo uma zi abantu, zi bonwa ekungeneni kwazo end*hl*ini; a zi vami ukungena ngomnyango. Kumbe zi ngena ku nge ko 'muntu, z' enyuke zi y' emsamo, zi *hl*ale kona, zi zibute. I nga li d*hl*i isele nempuku, i *hl*ale nje, i ze i bonwe umuntu, a bize abanye; i ng' etuki ukubaleka, i ze i shiywe nje. Abanye ba ti, "A i bulawe." Abanye ba ti, "Umuntu lo?"

Uma i nenxeba o*hl*angotini, a vele ow' azi ubanibani wakona owafayo, a taho ukuti, "Ubani lo. A ni li boni inxeba leli o*hl*angotini na?" I yekwe ke. Ku lalwe.

Ku ti ebusuku umninimuzi a pupe ipupo ukuti, "Ni se ni funa uku ngi bulala nje? Se ni ko*hl*iwe ini imina na? Nga ti, ngi zokcela ukud*hl*a; na ngi bulala na? Ngi Ubani."

Ku se kusasa e wa lauza lawo 'mapupo, a ti, "A ku ncencezwe ukuze itongo li nga tukuteli, li si bulale." Ku funwe inkomo, noma

Common people turn into the Umthlwazi, and chieftainesses. Another snake is called Ubulube or Inkwakwa, and another Umzingandhlu; common people turn into these only.

These snakes are known to be human beings when they enter a hut; they do not usually enter by the doorway. Perhaps they enter when no one is there, and go to the upper part of the hut, and stay there coiled up. A snake of this kind does not eat frogs or mice; it remains quiet, until some one sees it and calls others; it is not afraid so as to run away, and it is left alone. Some say, "Let it be killed." Others say, "What, kill a man?"

If the snake has a scar on the side, someone, who knew a certain dead man of that place who also had such a scar, comes forward and says, "It is So-and-so. Do you not see the scar on his side?" It is left alone, and they go to sleep.

During the night the chief of the village dreams, and the dead man says to him, "Do you now wish to kill me? Do you already forget me? I thought I would come and ask for food; and do you kill me? I am So-and-so."

In the morning he tells his dreams, and says, "Let a sin-offering be sacrificed, lest the Itongo be angry and kill us." They fetch a bullock or goat; and pray

imbuzi, ku bongwe, ku d*h*liwe. Ku k*q*abukwe i nga se ko. Se i te nya.

Inyoka nje i ngena end*h*lini, i talaze, y esab' abantu; i bulawe, ngoba i y' aziwa ukuba umlaland*h*le.

Futi i y' aziwa na ngok*q*obo lwayo nje, ukuba isilwane, i bulawe noma i nga talazi, ngokuba a i si yo imamba e ku tiwa umuntu, nenyandezulu i y' aziwa ukuba umuntu. Z' a*h*lukene ezi abantu nezi nge 'bantu ngombala wazo. Njengebululu nevuzamanzi nen*h*langwana nemamba empofu, nelu*h*laza i namabala, zi y' aziwa lezo ukuba imilaland*h*le. A kw enzeki ukuba i be umuntu ngesinye isikati; a zi penduki; zi imilaland*h*le njalo. Nezi abantu zi abantu njalo; zi bonwa k*q*ede, ku tiwe abantu; nembala zi kulume ngamapupo; noma zi nga kulumi, kw aziwe ukuba umuntu.

Ukwaziwa kwazo lezo ezi abantu z' aziwa ngokujwayela ekaya, na ngokungad*h*li izimpuku, nokungetuki umsindo wabantu; zi bonwe njalo i ng' etuki isitunzi somuntu, i ng' esabeki kubantu, ku nga bi

and eat the flesh. They look, and the snake is no longer there. It has now entirely disappeared.

A mere snake, when it comes into a hut, looks from side to side, and is afraid of men; and it is killed because it is known to be a wild snake.

A snake is also known by its mere appearance to be an animal, even though it does not look from side to side, because it is neither an Imamba[53] that is a man, nor the Inyandezulu,[54] which is known to be a man. Those which are men and those which are not, are distinguished by their colour. The Puffadder, the Ivuzamanzi, the Inthlangwana, and the grey and spotted Imamba, are known to be mere beasts. It is impossible for them to be ever men; they never become men; they are always beasts. And those which are men are always men; as soon as they are seen they are known to be men; and truly they speak in dreams; and even if they do not, it is known that they are men.

Those which are men are known by their frequenting huts, and by their not eating mice, and by their not being frightened at the noise of men; they are always observed not to be afraid of the shadow of a man; neither does a snake that is an Itongo excite fear in men,

[53] That is, the black imamba.

[54] Or green imamba. There is besides a spotted green, and grey Imamba.

ko nesitunzi end*hl*ini sokuba ku kona isilwane, ku pole nje, ku zwakale ukuba ku fike umninimuzi. Ekuboneni kwabantu ku nga ti ngoku i bona nje i ya kuluma ukuti, "Ni ng' esabi. Umina." Ba tola 'mand*hl*a njalo uku*hl*angana nayo.

Uma i bulewe umuntu o ng' aziyo, i buye i vuke, i fike nazo izinduku lezo e b' i bulawa ngazo, zi semzimbeni imivimbo; i kulume ngepupo, i sola ukupatwa kabi kwayo. Ku ncencezwe emva kwaloko. I loko ke e z' aziwa ngako izinyoka.

Ku ti owa e nesikci emzimbeni, a bonwe ngaso; nekcide li bonwe ngeso enyokeni; nengozi i bonwe ngayo; nonyonga lu bonwe ngako. Zi bonwa ngaloko ke, ngokuba abantu imvamo ba vame ukuba nezikci, izinyoka zabo zi njalo. Aba nge nazikci ba ya kuluma. Noma ku bonwa ukuba itongo, kodwa e nge nasikci, ku tiwe, "Umuntu lo;" kodwa a si m azi. A ziveze ngokukuluma. Z' aziwa ngaloko ke.

Futi, uma inyoka e itongo i lala

and there is no feeling of alarm as though there was a wild beast in the house; but there is a happy feeling, and it is felt that the chief of the village has come. When men see it, it is as though it said as they look at it, "Be not afraid. It is I." So they are able at all times to associate with it.

If it has been killed by someone who is ignorant, it comes to life again, and has the marks of the rod on its body by which it was killed; and complains in a dream of the treatment it has received. And after that a sin-offering is sacrificed. This, then, is how snakes are distinguished.

He who had a scar is recognised by that; and he who had but one eye is recognised by the snake into which he has turned having one eye also; and another is recognised by the marks of injuries; and a lame man is known by the lameness of the snake. That is how they are known, for men usually have some marks, and the snakes into which they turn have similar marks. The man who had no mark speaks in dreams. And if it is seen that it is an Itongo, but it has no mark, it is said to be a man, but we do not know who it is. He reveals himself by speaking. This is how they are known.

Again, if a snake which is an

ngom*hl*ana, i bekise isisu pezulu, ku y' esabeka, ku tiwa inkulu indaba e za 'uvela—noma, ku za 'ububa umuzi. Ku keolwe, ku yiwe enyangeni yokubula, i ku lande loko okwenziwa itongo ngako; ku lungiswe.

Itongo lies on its back, with its belly upwards, it is a cause of alarm, and it is said something of consequence is about to happen,—or, the village is about to be destroyed. The people sacrifice and pray, and go to a diviner, and he tells them why the Itongo has done as it has. They do as they are directed.

Uma i tandela isitsha, i y' ala ukuba si tabatwe, ku ze ku funwe into, ku tetwe, i suke.

If a snake coils around a vessel and will not allow any one to take it, the people bring a sacrifice and worship, and it goes away.

Futi, uma inyoka e itongo i ngena ngen*hl*uzula, kw aziwe ukuba itongo lomuntu owa e ihhatanga e sa pila. U sa hamba ngako ukwenza kwake. Ku lungiswe ngento.

And if a snake which is an Itongo enters a house rapidly,[55] it is known to be the Itongo of a man who was a liar whilst he lived. And he is still a liar. They sacrifice something to such an Itongo.

I loko ke e ngi kw aziyo ngamatongo.

UMPENGULA MBANDA.

This is what I know about the Amatongo.

Men turn into many kinds of Animals.

KU tiwa abantu ba penduka izilwane eziningi. Omunye ku tiwa u ba umnyovu; omunye a be isalukazana; nomunye imamba; nomunye inyandezulu; imvamo ba

IT is said that men turn into many kinds of animals. It is said that one becomes a wasp; another an isalukazana;[56] another an imamba;[57] another an inyandezulu;[58] but the greater number turn into

---

[55] Rapidly, or rather, without any shame,—arbitrarily, as one that has a right to do as he likes, whose will is his law.

[56] *Isalukazana*, a kind of lizard.

[57] *Imamba*, a poisonous snake.

[58] *Inyandezulu*, a poisonous snake, the green imamba.

penduka umhlwazi oluhlaza nonsundu. Leyo 'mihlwazi yombili umuntu a nga ze a vume, a ti, "Yebo, abantu laba," e tsho ngokuba i nga twali 'mehlo njengalezo 'zilwanyana ezine. A w esabi umhlwazi umuntu, u hamba kahle; uma umuntu e u bona u lele, ku ze ku fike abaningi ba u bone; noma be u vusa, u ti siki, u me.

Ngaloko ke ku tiwa, u itongo, ngokuba a u bonanga u luma 'muntu; isilwane e si nge nalulaka kuzo zonke. Oluhlaza nonsundu i ya fana ngokuba-mnene.

Kepa ezinye, noma ku tiwa zi amatongo, kepa a zi jwayeleki emehlweni, ngokuba lu uhlobo lwezilwane ezi lumako. A i bonakali imamba yasenhle neyasekaya ngombala; umbala wayo munye, amehlo ayo manye; neyasenhle ukubheka kwayo kunye—ukubheka kwempi okwesabisa umuntu; a nga melwa isibindi ukuti, "Itongo. Ngi nga sondela kuyo." Ai; u tsho e kude e nga sondeli. Kodwa

the umthlwazi,[59] which may be green or brown. As regards the two kinds of umthlwazi, a person may allow that they are men, because they do not stare fiercely like the other four. The umthlwazi is not afraid of a man, it moves slowly; if a person sees it lying, it remains quiet until many come and look at it; and if they arouse it, it moves slightly, and again remains quiet.

Therefore it is said to be an Itongo, for it never bites any one; it is a beast which is less fierce than all others. The green and brown kinds resemble each other in gentleness.

And the others, although they are called Amatongo, yet the eyes do not get accustomed to them,[60] for they belong to a kind of animal which bites. The imamba which frequents open places, and those which frequent houses, are not distinguishable by colour; their colour is the same, their eyes are alike; and when they are in an open place, their stare is of the same character—the stare of an enemy, which makes one afraid; and a man does not pluck up courage by saying, "This snake is an Itongo. I can approach it." No; he says it is an Itongo when he is at a distance from it, without

[59] *Umhlwazi*, a harmless snake.

[60] They do not become common in the eyes, that is, so as to be approached familiarly,—the eyes do not get accustomed to them.

emhlwazini si tsho, si sondela kuwo.

approaching near to it. But we say the umthlwazi is an Itongo, and go up to it.

Kakulu imamba ku tiwa amakosi; kepa izalukazana ku tiwa abafazi abadala; umhlwazi ku tiwa abantu. Umnyovu a ku tshiwo ngokubonakalako, ukuti u itongo, ngokuba u vela emntwini; ku nga u itongo ngokutunywa; i ilo ngokubonwa kwawo ke, ku tiwe, u itongo; ngokuba ku tiwa ngawo, ku nga u isitunywa.

But the imamba is said especially to be chiefs; the isalukazana, old women; and the umthlwazi, common people. As regards the wasp, it is not clear that it is an Itongo, because it appears to a man; it is as it were an Itongo because it is sent; it is an Itongo through being seen, and so it is said to be an Itongo; for people say of it, it resembles something that has been sent.

The order in which the Amatongo are worshipped.

Ku ya bizwa amatongo onke ngetongo lokukqala el' aziwayo. Li bizwe njengaloku isizwe, ku tiwa, esakwabani; esetu ku tiwa samapepete. Isibongo ku tiwa Gwala, umuntu wokukqala, ukuti, unkulunkulu wamapepete. Uyena e inhloko yesizwe sonke; si kuleka ngaye. Ku ti uma ku hlatshwe, ku tiwe, "Nina'bakwagwala, pelela ni nonke, ni ze 'kudhla. Naku 'kudhla kwenu."

All the Amatongo are called upon by the name of the first Itongo who is known. It is called just as a nation is called after a certain person; ours is the nation of the Amapepete. The family name is Gwala, the first man, that is, the Unkulunkulu of the Amapepete. It is he who is the head of the whole nation; we pray by his name. And when we sacrifice we say, "Ye people of Gwala, come all of you to eat. Behold your food."

Kepa manje ngokuba ku kona izinyanga, a ku sa kqalwa ngaloko; ngokuba kwabafayo u y' aziwa oyena e ngenise isifo; w' aziwa

But now since there are diviners we no longer begin in this way; for it is known who among the dead has caused disease; he is

ngokubula ezinyangeni, ukuba, "Ubani lowo u gula nje, u bulawa Ubani lowo wakini. Ni ya m azi; u ti, ku ngani ukuba ku ti lapa ni pete ukudhla ni nga m kumbuli na?" Ngaloko ke ku ya bizwa yena kukqala, ku tiwe, "Bani kabani," e bongwa ngezibongo zake; ku ze ku fikwe na kuyise, a ngeniswe naye kule 'ndaba yokufa; ku ze ku fikwe kwowokupela; se ku ya gcinwa ke uma ku tiwa, "Nina 'bakwagwala, owa ti wa ti" (ku balwa izibongo zake), "pelela ni nonke."

known by enquiring of the diviners; they tell us, "Since So-and-so is ill, he is made ill by So-and-so, one of your people. You know him; he says, how is it that when you have food you forget him?" Therefore he is called upon first, and it is said, "So-and-so, son of So-and-so," he being lauded by his laud-giving names; then they proceed to his father, and he too is mentioned in connection with the disease; and so in time they come to the last; and so there is an end, when it is said, "Ye people of Gwala, who did so and so" (his great deeds being mentioned), "come all of you."

Ku njalo ke ukwahlukanisa amatongo. 'Ahlukaniswa ngokuba u ba munye ematongweni o yena e veza isifo. Abanye ba nga tsho 'luto. Ku bizwe yena ke kukqala, njengokuba e kala ngokuti, "Ku ngani ukuba ngi nga be ngi sa patwa na?" Ku njalo ke.

Such then is the distinction between Amatongo. They are distinguished, because it is one among them which causes the disease. The others say nothing. So he is called upon first, as though he complained saying, "How is it that my name is no longer mentioned?" That is how it is.

Njengaloku kwiti, kwa ka kwa gula ubabekazi; kwa tiwa ezinyangeni, "U bulawa umfo wabo, ngokuti, 'Kulo 'muzi, noma ku petwe ukudhla, a ngi sa kunjulwa;' e tsho, ngokuti, 'Ku ngani ukuba ku nga kqalwa ngaye ukubizwa ematongweni onke na?'"

Just as with us, our uncle was ill; the diviners said, "He is made ill by his brother, because he says, 'In that village when they have food, I am no longer remembered;' and he asks, 'How is it that you do not begin with him when you call on the Amatongo?'"

Amatongo a sa hlupa abantu ngaloko. Ilelo li ya banga njalo,

The Amatongo continually trouble men on that account. Each

ukuze onke a be nezinkomo zawo, noma e patwa onke. Kepa otile u kumbula ngokuti, "Mina, a ba bonanga be ngi pata kuk*q*ala uku ngi *hl*abela inkomo etile; ngi za 'uziveza ngokufa."

one of them constantly puts in a claim, that each may have his own cattle [sacrificed for him individually], though the names of all be called upon. And a certain one remembers they never worship him first by killing for him a certain cow; and he says, "I will reveal myself by disease."

I njalo ke indaba yokwa*hl*ukanisa amatongo.

UMPENGULA MBANDA.

This then is the word about making a distinction between the Amatongo.

Tale of an Imamba.

INDABA yemamba e itongo lakwiti emapepeteni. Inkosi yakona Umaziya. Leyo 'nkosi ya penduka imamba ekupumeni emzimbeni wobuntu. Ya bulawa embo. Kwa ti ekukciteken kwezwe lakwazulu, abantu ba tanda ukuza lapa esilungwini. Kepa yona ya se i file. Indodana yayo Umyeka owa sala esikund*hl*eni sikayise, nomfo wabo Umgwaduyana wa fa yena, wa shiya amadodana amabili, enye Umadikane, enye encane, Ubafako.

THE account of the Imamba which is the Itongo of our people among the Amapepete. The chief of that nation was Umaziya.[61] That chief became an Imamba when he went out of his human body. He was killed by the Abambo. When the people were scattered from the country of the Amazulu, they wished to come here to the English. But he had been dead for some time. It was his son, Umyeka, who remained in his father's place, and his brother too, Umgwaduyana, died, and left two sons, one named Umadikane, and the younger one, Ubafako.

Kepa ngaleso 'sikati sokukciteka kwezwe, lowo 'mfana wa e nesilonda esibi etangeni; kepa se ku

But at the time of the scattering of the people the lad Ubafako had a bad sore on his thigh; they

[61] *Umaziya.*—The z pronounced like z in azure.

hanjiwe en*h*le, ku punyiwe emakaya, e gula kakulu ileso 'silonda; se kw elatshiwe ngemiti; kepa imiti i nga namateli, si be loku si biba njalo. Ku ze kwa ti ngolunye usuku, ku *h*leziwe emadokodweni okubaleka, kwa ngena imamba; loku umntwana u lele, abantu ba ng*q*azuka, b' etuka be bona isilwane si ngena end*h*lini; kepa a i ba nakanga nokwetuka nje, kupela ya pikelela ukwenyuka i ye kumntwana; unina e se kala e ti, "Inyoka i ya 'kud*h*la umntwana."

were then living in the open country and had quitted their homes, when he was ill with that sore; and it had been already treated with medicines; but the medicines would not adhere, and the sore increased continually. At length it happened one day, as they were living in the temporary booths erected in their flight, an Imamba entered; the child was asleep; the people started up and were frightened when they saw the beast enter the house; but it neither took any notice of them nor was in the least afraid, but pressed onward to go up to the child; the mother now cried out, "The snake will kill the child."

Kepa kwa se kw aziwa ukuba inkosi le; kepa a ba melwanga 'sibindi, ngokuba se i nomunye umzimba, a ba nga jwayelani nawo—umzimba wezilwane. Ya fika, ya beka umlomo esilondeni, kwa ba isikatshana i tulisile, y' esuka, ya puma.

But it was already known that it was the chief; but they had not any courage on that account, for he had now a different body, to which they were not accustomed,—the body of a beast. It reached the child and placed its mouth on the sore, and remained still a little while, and then departed and went out of the house.

Ku ti ngemva kwaloko kwa yiwa ezinyangeni, ukuba ku zwakale ukuba lo 'm*h*lola ongaka wemamba ini na. Kepa za ti zona izinyanga, "Inkosi yakwini leyo; i zokwelapa umntwana wendodana yayo."

After that they went to the diviners, that they might hear what was the meaning of so great an omen. But the doctors said, "It is your chief; he comes to heal the child of his son."

Nembala ke kwa *h*laliwa; isilonda sa buya, sa za sa pola.

So the people waited in patience; and the sore contracted, and at length healed.

Ku be ku ti lapa ku hanjwa, ku ziwa, lapa ku hanjiwe, nayo i bonwe lapa ku welwa emazibukweni; i be i wela ngenzansi njalo; kwa za kwa fikwa lapa emkambatini, lapa ya sala kona ngesikati sokwehla kwendodana, Umyeka, e ya enanda, e balekela Amabunu.

And it used constantly to happen, when they were travelling towards this country, when they had set out, the Imamba too was seen where they crossed at the fords of rivers; it used to cross lower down constantly; until they reached Table Mountain, where it still was when his son, Umyeka, went down to the Inanda, flying from the Dutch.

Kepa inkosi leyo y' ala, ya ti, "A ngi yi 'kuza ezweni lolwandhle. Ngi za 'kuhlala lapa, ngi zidhlele izintete nje." Nembala ke kwa ba njalo. Kwa za kwa gula Umyeka kakulu, e pupa ku tiwa, "Wa m shiyela ni uyihlo? U ya ba biza; u ti, a ba buye." Kepa a ba vumanga ngokwesaba umlanjwana wamabunu, ngokuba kwa dhliwa izinkomo zawo Umyeka.

But the chief[62] refused, saying, "I will not go to a country by the sea. I shall stay here, and eat grasshoppers."[63] And so indeed it was. At length Umyeka was very ill, and it was said to him in a dream, "Why did you forsake your father?[64] He is calling the people; let them return." But they would not agree, fearing their feud with the Dutch, for Umyeka had stolen their cattle.[65]

Kwa ba njalo ke, ku ze kwa kupuka omunye ubabekazi omkulu, e ya kubaba, ow' elamana no zala tina. W' esuka lowo 'baba, e dedela ubabekazi, wa buyela

So it was until our eldest uncle went up to our father,[66] who was younger than our own father. Our father departed, leaving our eldest uncle, and returned

---

[62] That is, the imamba,—the dead chief.

[63] It is to be understood that this was said to the son in a dream.

[64] That is, forsake the place where his Itongo revealed itself.

[65] It is supposed by the narrator that this tribe stole at least a thousand head of cattle from the Dutch.

[66] Both the Ubabakazi, eldest uncle, and the Ubaba, father, were uncles. There were three brothers. The eldest is here called Ubabakazi; the second, the father, was dead; the youngest, here called father, had charge of the family of the second.

enxiweni elikulu lenkosi yakwiti. Kodwa wa bhekana nalo; ka nge-nanga kulo; kwa linywa nje kulo. Ku ze kwa ti ngolunye usuku ubaba e lele wa pupa inkosi leyo i kuluma naye. Lokupela ngaleso 'sikati kwa ku sebusika, amanzi e banda kakulu, ya ti, "Ngqo-kqwane, ku*h*le ukuba u ng' enzele ikqamuka ezibukweni, ngi wele ngalo, ngi z' ekaya; ngokuba ngi ya godola amakaza, ngi bandwa na amanzi futi."

to the old site of our chief's great kraal. But he was on the other side of the stream to it; he did not build on the old site, bnt dug there only. Until on a certain day our father whilst asleep dreamt the chief was talking with him. And as at that time it was winter, and the water was very cold, he said to him, "Ungqo-kqwane, it would be well for you to make a bridge for me, that I may cross on it and come home; for I am cold, and the water makes me colder still."

Nembala ng' ezwa ubaba e se ngi biza, e ti, "Mntanami, woza, si ye lapaya ezibukweni eli ya enxiweni lasemzimvubu, umuzi wenkosi, si yokwenzela inkosi ko-na ikqamuka lokuwela." Nembala ke sa gaula iminga kakulu nemi-senge, sa i nqumisa kabili emfuleni, sa tela um*h*laba ngapezulu.

And truly I heard my father calling me and saying, "My child, come, let us go yonder to the ford which leads to the old site of Umzimvubu, the village of the chief, and make there a bridge for the chief to cross over." And truly we cut down many mimosa trees and elephant trees, and laid them across the stream, and poured earth on the top of them.

Ku ngezinsukwana lezo, loku-pela nga ngi umfana wezinkomo o vala isango, nga libala kakulu ukuya 'uvala, kwa za kwa *h*lwa; ngi te se ngi ya, nga ngi ya, se ku d*h*lule isikati sokuvala. Nga i bona ngi sa ya njeya into e kcwe-bezela emivalweni. Kepa a ngi nakanga ukuba ini. Nga ya nga-mand*h*la, ngi tanda ukuvala masi-

A few days after, for I was then the herd-boy who closed the cattle pen, I put off for a long time go-ing to close it, until it was dark; and did not set out to do it until the usual time had passed. As I was going, I saw yonder something glistening on the poles with which the gateway was closed. But I did not trouble myself as to what it was. I went in a hurry, wish-ing to close the gateway at once,

nyane, ngokuba nga shiya end*h*lini ku za 'ud*h*liwa amasi. Ngaloko ke nga tanda ukuvala masinyane. Kepa nga tata lowo 'mvalo; wa sinda, ng' a*h*luleka; na komunye kwa ba njalo; ya ng' a*h*lula imivalo. Nga k*q*ala ukubhekisisa ukuba nam*h*la nje imivalo i ngi sinda ngani, loku imivalo emidala nje na? Nga bhekisisa, kanti inyoka enkulu e lele pezu kwemivalo. Nga kala. Kwa punywa ekaya, kwa buzwa ini na? Nga ti, "Nansi inyoka."

for I left them about to eat amasi in the house. Therefore I wished to close the gateway at once. But I took the first pole; it was heavy, I could not raise it; and it was the same with another; the poles were too heavy for me. I began to examine intently into the cause why the poles were too heavy, since they were old poles. I looked intently, and forsooth it was a great snake which was lying on them. I shouted. They came out of the house, and asked what it was. I replied, "Here is a snake."

Ubaba wa fika masinyane, wa bhekisisa, wa ti, "Yeka ukuvala." Nga buza, nga ti, "Ini le na?" Wa ti, "Inkosi." Nga ti, "Inyoka le na?" Wa ti, "Yebo."

My father came immediately, and looked intently, and said, "Do not close the gateway." I enquired, "What is it?" He said, "It is the chief." I said, "What, this snake?" He said, "Yes."

Sa buyela end*h*lini. Ku te ku sa wa e si tshela, e ti, "Inkosi i ti, 'Ku ngani ukuba ni ng' etuke?' A ngi ti ya tsho ya ti, a kw enziwe ind*h*lela, i za 'kuza na?"

We returned to the house. In the morning he told us, saying, "The chief asks why you were afraid of him. Did he not tell us to make a bridge, that he might cross?"

Kwa ba se ku ya bongwa ke ubaba, e bonga inyoka leyo ngezibongo zayo inkosi i sa hamba; be bonga nomamemkulu o zala ubaba. Ngokuba kwiti ku njalo. Itongo li *h*lala kumuntu omkulu, li kulume naye; noma ku bongwa ekaya,

Then my father gave praises, praising the snake with the laud-giving names which the chief had whilst living; praising in concert with our grandmother, the mother of my father. For such is the custom with us. The Itongo dwells with the great man, and speaks with him; and when worship is performed at a house, it is the

ku bonga indoda enkulu nesalukazi esidala es' aziyo abantu a se ba fa.

Kwa ba njalo ke, kwa za kwa kupuka umuzi wenkosi omunye, w' eza lapa si kona. Loku ku ze kwa fika Ungoza, wa si kipa ngezwi likasomseu. Sa kciteka, sa ya ezindaweni eziningi. Nanso ke into e nga i bonako. I leyo ke.

Kwa ti ngemva kwaloko ya kupuka inkosi, Umyeka. Ku tiwa, "A ku yiwe enziweni, ku yiwe 'kubiza inkosi, uyise wenkosi; ngokuba kwa tiwa, umuzi u buba nje, ngokuba inkosi i nga vumanga ukwe*h*la." Nembala ke kwa fikwa nenkomokazi, ikolokazi, ntambama; se ku *h*langaniswa izikulu zonke zamadoda namake*h*la. Kw' enziwa igama likayise lomkosi, uku m vusa uku m kumbuza ukuba, "Nembala ba ya *h*lupeka abantwana bami, ngokuba ngi nge ko kubo." I leli ke igama ela *h*latshelelwa, lokuti:—

"Limel' u *h*lole amazimw[67] etu asesiwandiye.

chief man, and the oldest old woman, who knew those who are dead, who worship.

Under these circumstances, one of the chief's kraal at length came up to where we were living; and we lived together till Ungoza came and turned us out by the direction of Usomseu. We were scattered, and went to other places. That, then, is a thing which I saw.

After that Umyeka, the chief, came up. The people said, "Let us go to the old dwelling to call the chief, the present chief's father; for the village is perishing because the chief did not consent to go down to the coast." So then they brought a dun-coloured cow in the afternoon; and all the chief men, both old and young, were assembled. They sang a song of their father which used to be sung on great festivals, to arouse him to the recollection that his children were truly in trouble because he was not among them. This is the song which was sung:—

"Dig for[68] the chief, and watch our gardens which are at Isiwandiye.[69]

---

[67] Amazimu *for* amasimu; the z being used for s to give weight to the sound; the u changed into w before the vowel in the following word.

[68] *Limel'*—dig for, not known for whom, but probably, as here translated, the chief.

[69] *Asesiwandiye*—Isiwandiye *for* Isiwandile. The name of a place, as if of a place where there were many gardens.

"Amanga lawo.
Limel' u *h*lole amazimw etu asesiwandiye.
Amanga lawo.
Asesiwandiye, I-i-i-zi—asesiwandiye.
Amanga lawo."

Kw' enziwa umkumbu omkulu ngapand*h*le kwenziwa. Kwa gujwa, loku se ku pelele abafazi notshwala nezintombi. Kwa za kwa kcitekwa, se li tshona, izulu se li na; kwa yiwa ekaya emzini wakwiti, lokupela utshwala bu y' esabeka ubuningi; kwa d*h*liwa ke utshwala nenyama, kwa kcwaywa umkcwayo.

Ku te ku se njalo kwa puma omunye o ike*h*la; ku tiwa Uma*h*lati ibizo lake; u t' e buya wa e tsho ukuba "Inkosi se i fikile, si kcwaya nje. Nansi lapa se i butene kona pezu kwend*h*lu." Kwa boboswa ind*h*lu pezulu, ukuze i buke umkcwayo. Kwa kcwaywa kwa za kwa nga ku nga sa ngokujabula okukulu, ukuba ku tiwa, "Id*h*lozi lakwiti li *h*langene nati namu*h*la; umuzi u za 'kuma." Kwa ba njalo ke. Ukupela ke kwendaba leyo.

"Those words are naught.[70]
Dig for the chief, and watch our gardens which are at Isiwandiye.
Those words are naught.
Which are at Isiwandiye, I-i-i-zi[71]—which are at Isiwandiye.
Those words are naught."

A large circle was formed outside the old site. They danced. There were there also all the women with beer, and the damsels. At length they separated when the sun was going down and it was raining, and they went home to our village, for the abundance of beer was fearful; so they consumed beer and meat, and sang hut-songs.[72]

In the midst of these doings, one of the young men, named Umathlati, went out; on his return he said, "The chief has come, even whilst we are singing. There he is, coiled up on the house." A hole was made in the house, that he might look on at the singing. They sang until it was near morning, rejoicing exceedingly because it was said, "The Idhlozi of our people has now united with us; our village will stand." Thus then it was. That is the end of the tale.

---

[70] *Those words are naught,*—that is, we object to dig at Isiwandile.

[71] *I-i-i-zi.*—Z in zi pronounced as in azure. This chorus is used for the purpose of emphatically asserting the subject of the song.

[72] The *umkcwayo* is a song which is sung in the hut, the singers sitting, and accompanying the song with regulated motions of the body.

Kepa lapa ya i *h*lala kona leyo 'nyoka, i b' i *h*lala otangweni esibayeni; kumbe na send*h*lini enkulu; ngokuba ku be ku tiwa izinyoka eziningi pakati kwomuzi kwaleyo 'nd*h*lu enkulu, ku tiwa amanxusa enkosi, a hamba nenkosi; ku tshiwo abantu aba fa nayo. Ngemva kwaloko ke ya nyamalala ekufikeni kwomuzi wenkosi; a ya be i sa vama ukubonwa lapo, i bonwe ngesinye isikati, ku be ukupela.

And the place where the snake stayed was in the fence of the cattle-pen; and it may be even in the great house; and it was said that the many snakes which were in the village belonging to the great house, were the chief's attendants which accompanied him; they were said to be the men who were killed at the same time as the chief. After that he disappeared on the arrival of the chief's kraal; and was no longer seen frequently at our kraal, but only occasionally.

Imamba itongo lend*h*lu 'nkulu; abantu nje a ba penduki imamba, ba penduka imi*h*lwazi, inyoka elu*h*laza, im*h*lope ngapansi, ikanjana layo lincane. Ukuma kwayo, i bheka umuntu, a i bhekisi kwesilwane es' esaba ukubulawa, i bheka ka*h*le nje; ku nga butana abantu abaningi kuwo um*h*lwazi. Kepa noma umuntu e u tinta ngento u nga baleki, u gud*h*luka nje. Um*h*lwazi isidanda esikulu ezinyokeni; end*h*lini u hamb' ind*h*lu yonke, a w esabi 'ndawo, na pezulu u ya bonakala, na sezingutsheni u *h*lale; umuntu a tate ka*h*le ingubo yake, a u shiye pansi, u ng' enzi 'luto. Ku tiwa u itongo.

UMPENGULA MBANDA.

The imamba is the Itongo of the great house; the common people do not become izimamba, they become imithlazi; this snake is green and white on its belly, and has a very small head. Its custom is, when looking at a man, not to look like an animal which fears to be killed; it looks without alarm; and many people may gather around an umthlazi. And even if a man touches it with a stick, it does not run away, but just moves. The umthlwazi is much tamer than other snakes; it moves about the whole house, and fears nothing, and it is seen in the roof, and it remains among the garments; and a man takes up his garment gently and leaves the snake on the ground, and it does nothing. It is said to be an Itongo.

Removing from one country to another.

Ku ti uma ku za 'usukwa ku yiwe kwelinye izwe, uma ku bonwa ukuba itongo a ba li boni kulo 'muzi omutsha, la sal' emuva, ku gaulwe ihlahla lompafa, kumbe ku yiwe nenkomo, ku ye 'kuhlatshwa kona enxiweni, ku bongwe, li bizwe, kw enziwe amahhubo a e hhuba ngawo e sa hamba; loko isibonakaliso soku m kalela, ukuvusa umunyu, ngokuti, "Nembala, abanta bami ba nesizungu uma be nga ngi boni." Ku hholwe ihlahla lapa se ku hanjwa, ku yiwe nalo lapa ku yiwe kona. Kumbe i landele; kumbe y ale ngamazwi e nga tandi ngawo ukuya kuleyo 'ndawo, i kuluma nendodana ngepupa; kumbe nomuntu omdala walo 'muzi; noma inkosikazi endala.

When we are about to go to another country, if the people do not see the Itongo at the new village, it having staid behind, a branch of umpafa is cut, and perhaps they take a bullock with them, and go to sacrifice it at the old site; they give thanks, and call on the Itongo, and sing those songs which he used to sing whilst living; this is a sign of weeping for him, to excite pity, so that he may say, "Truly, my children are lonely because they do not see me." And the branch is dragged when they set out, and they go with it to the new village. Perhaps the snake follows; perhaps it refuses, giving reasons why it does not wish to go to that place, speaking to the eldest son in a dream; or it may be to an old man of the village; or the old queen.

Royal Attendants.

Amanxusa abantu benkosi njengezinceku, aba hamba nayo; ku ti noma se i file inkosi, kakulu uma i bulawa, i bulawa namanxusa, ukuze a i lungisele pambili, nokudhla a i funele. Kakulu kiti ku

Amanxusa are people of a chief like servants, who go about in company with him; and even when the chief is dead, and especially if he has been killed together with his Amanxusa, they go with him, that they may prepare things before hand, and get food for him. It was especially the

be ku ti endulo, uma ku fe inkosi, i nga fi yodwa; lokupela be be tshiswa abantu kukqala; se i file inkosi, ngamhla i pum' ekaya, se i ya 'ulahlwa, ku hlonywe izihlangu, ku vunulwe kakulu imvunulo yempi. Ku ti uma ku fikwe endaweni lapa inkosi i za 'utshiswa kona, ku gaulwe izinkuni eziningi; loku nezinkabi zi kona futi, ku ti inkabi yayo e dhlala umkosi ngayo i hlatshwe nayo, kunye nayo, i fe njengayo. Ku ti uma umlilo u vuta, i fakwe; ku be se ku ketwa izinceku zayo, zi i landele; ku landwe izikulu, zi tatwe ngazinye. Ku tiwe, "Ubani u fanele a hambe nenkosi." Ku ti lapa umlilo u kqala ukulota, ku tiwe, "Kwezela, 'bani." A ti lapa e ti u hlanganisa izikuni, ba m fake kona; zonke izikulu ku hambe ku tatwa ngabanye ezindhlini ezinkulu zomdeni naba nge 'mdeni; ku fe abantu abaningi ngalelo 'langa. Nanko ke amanxusa.

case with us at first, when a chief died, he did not die alone; for at first the bodies of the dead were burnt, and when a chief died, and they went from their home to dispose of the remains, they took shields and adorned themselves with their military ornaments; and when they came to the place where the remains of the chief were to be burnt, they cut down much firewood; and as there were oxen there too, the chief ox with which he made royal festivals was killed with him, that it might die with him. When the fire was kindled, the chief was put in; and then his servants were chosen, and put into the fire after the chief; the great men followed, they were taken one by one. They said, "So-and-so is fit to go with the chief." When the fire began to sink down, they said, "Put the fire together, So-and-so." And when he was putting the firewood together, they cast him in; they went and took all the great men one by one from the chief houses of the chief's brothers, and from those who were not his brothers. Many people were killed on that day. Such then are the Amanxusa.

Ku be se ku ti uma inkosi i file ba tubelise abantwana babo; abanye ngokuti, "Ngi y' azi ukuba uma ngi vumela ukuba umntanami

When a chief dies the people conceal their children; some saying, "I know that if I let my

a ye lapa ku fele inkosi kona, ka sa yi 'kubuya." Ba vame uku ba tubelisa. Nokugula futi abanye ba zigulise, ba bikwe kakulu, ku tiwe, "Ubani a si ko nako ukufa."

child go to the place where the king has died, he will never come back again." So they usually conceal them. Others too feign sickness, and cause the report of their sickness to be spread abroad in all directions; they say, "So-and-so is very ill indeed."

I ti uma i tshe i ti du, ku be se ku tatwa umlota wonke, u ye u telwe esizibeni.

When the chief is entirely consumed, they take the ashes and throw them into a pool of the river.

Aman*x*usa abantu aba be konza Utshaka. Ku ti emva kwokufa kwake zonke izikulu zake eza zi m konza, za ti uba zi fe za *h*langana naye ukuya 'u m konza. Ku tiwa ku kona izinyoka eziningi; lezo 'nyoka ku tiwa aman*x*usa; zi kona kwazulu; ku ti lapa ku bonwa Utshaka, nazo zi be zi kona; ngokuba ku tiwa u imamba enkulu; u ya bonwa ngezikati zonke e landelwa izinyoka; ku tiwe aman*x*usa ake. Ngesinye isikati ku tiwa wa ka wa bonwa e lwa nodingane, lapa se be file bobabili; ba lwa isikati eside; kwa za kwa puma impi eningi ukuya 'ku ku bona loko 'kulwa. Ku tiwa Umpande wa tanda ukwelamulela Utshaka, a bulale Udingane, ngokuba wa e tanda uku m bulala; wa sinda ngond*h*lela.

Aman*x*usa are men who used to wait upon Utshaka. And after his death all the great men who used to wait on him, when they died, joined him that they might wait on him. It is said there are many snakes among the Amazulu; these snakes are Aman*x*usa; when Utshaka is seen, then too are seen the snakes; for it is said he is a large imamba; he is seen continually, followed by snakes; and they are all said to be Aman*x*usa. It is said that he was once seen fighting with Udingane, when both were dead; they fought a long time, until at length a very great number went out to see the fight. It is said Umpande wished to help Utshaka and kill Udingane, because Udingane had wished to kill Umpande, but Undhlela[73] saved him.

Aman*x*usa a *h*lala end*h*lini en-

The Aman*x*usa remain in the

[73] An officer under Udingane.

kulu kwabo kankosi kwiti omapepeteni. Amanxusa a be hlala endhlini kasokane, umuntu omkulu. Owesifazana ngolunye usuku a ti, "Ngi ya hlupeka. Ngesinye isikati ngi kohlwa nokubeka izitsha nje, ngi vinjelwa izinyoka." Aba z' aziyo lezo 'nyoka ba ti, "Amanxusa enkosi; abantu aba be hamba nayo inkosi."

UMPENGULA MBANDA.

chief house of our chief among the Amapepete. The Amanxusa used to remain in Usokane's[74] house, a great man. One day a woman said, "I am troubled. I am sometimes unable even to put down a vessel, there being always snakes in the way." Those who knew them said, "They are Amanxusa of the chief; people who were living with the chief before he died."

Izalukazana.

ISALUKAZANA ku tiwa itongo lomuntu wesifazana owa e se gugile.

Ku kona indaba ngesalukazana, isilwanyana esi fana nentulwa; kepa si nge si yo; si uhlobo lwesibankhwa; kepa isibankhwa sibutshelezi, sinsundu ngapezulu, ngapansi ku nga simhlope. Kepa leso 'salukazana sibana, si ihhambana kakulu; a si tandeki; kepa si lulana, si tshetsha ukusuka masinyane. Kepa a si vami ukubaleka, si vama ukukcatsha. Ku ti uma umuntu e si bona ngalapa, si be se si ti bande ngalapaya. Uma u ya ngakona, si pambane nawe. Uma u si bone kukqala, sa tshetsha ukwebanda. Uma u kombisa umuntu, u ti, "Isilwanyana ngi si bone lapa," se si te site ngalapaya. A nga ti, "A si

THE lizard is said to be the Itongo of an old woman.

There is a tale about the isalukazana, an animal which resembles the intulwa; but it is not an intulwa; it is a kind of isibankhwa; but the isibankhwa is smooth, and purple on its back, and whitish on its belly. But the isalukazana is rather ugly, and very rough; it is not liked; and it is active, and runs away quickly. But it does not commonly run away, but hides itself. And if a man sees it on this side of any thing, it at once goes round to the opposite side. If you see it first, it makes haste to go round to the other side. If you point it out to another, saying, "I saw an animal here," it is already hidden on the other side. He may say, "Let us look;" but

---

[74] A very old man, who had grown up with Umaziya, the king.

bheke;" kepa si bone isitunzi somuntu si vela, si penduke, si pambane naso. A nga ze a ku pikise, a ti, "Ku njani ukuba umdala kangaka u k*q*amba 'manga na?" A ze a be isiula lowo o be si bonile, ngokuba emva ka sa si boni. Ba nga ze ba si bone uma b' a*h*lukana, omunye 'eme, omunye a zungeze umuti; ba si bone ke; lapa si balekela omunye, si vele ngakomunye.

it sees the shadow of the man as soon as it appears, and turns back in the opposite direction. Until he disputes, saying, "How is it that one so old as you tells lies?" And the one who saw it appears foolish, for he no longer sees it. They may see it if they separate, and one stands still, and the other goes round the tree; for so they see it; when it runs away from one of them, it appears to the other.

Ku ti uma si funwa end*h*lini, si te kcatsha otingweni, noma u sensikeni; omdala a si bone kumbe, a nga tsho 'luto, a nga tandi ukwandisa indaba; ngokuba ku tiwa mubi umuntu emdala a bone into e njengom*h*lola. U *h*lup' abantu; ba ya 'kutshaywa izinvalo, ba *h*lale be kcabanga ngaleyo 'nto e boniweko. Ku ti uma ku vela umkuba omubi pakati kwomuzi, leso 'salukazana si nga yekile ukubonakala kuleyo 'ndawo, ku tiwe i sona si bika ukufa. A i zeke ke indaba lo owa si bonako, a ti, "Kunsuku ngi bona isalukazana kamabani. Nga ngi ti, a ku yi 'kuvela 'luto; nga i fi*h*la leyo 'ndaba. Kepa loku naku se ku vele umkuba, ku*h*le kw aziwe."

If it is seen in the house, it hides itself among the wattles, or it may be on the post of the house; perhaps an old person sees it, but says nothing, not wishing to make much of the affair; for they say an old person is wicked if he see a thing which is like an omen. He troubles the people; they will be smitten with fear, and continue to think of that which has been seen. If something bad happens in the village, the isalukazana is seen continually in the same place, and it is said to prognosticate death. Then he who saw it says, "For some days I have seen an isalukazana in So-and-so's hut. I said nothing will come of it; and hid what I had seen. But now since the evil has come, it is proper that it should be known."

Abanye ba ti, "A ku yobulwa." Abanye ba ti, "Ku sa funwa ni? loku naku umhlola se u vele nje

Some say, "Let us go to the diviner." Others say, "What do we want? See, there is the omen

na? Ku*hl*e ku funwe into uma i kona, leso 'salukazana si kwotshwe si muke." Nembala ke ku *hl*atshwe imbuzi, noma itole.

come of its own accord. It is proper to get something if there is such a thing, to send away the isalukazana." And so they sacrifice a goat or a calf.

Ku tiwa isalukazana ukubizwa kwalezo 'zilwanyazana. A ku tshiwo itongo lendoda nelabantwana; ku tiwa itongo lomuntu wesifazana owa e se gugile. Futi a ku tshiwo ukuti ubani igama lake. Isalukazana njalo ukubizwa kwaso; a s' aziwa uma isalukazana esi unobani igama laso.

These animals are called isalukazana [little old women]. It is not said to be the Itongo of a man or of a child; but the Itongo of some old woman. Neither is it called by the name of any particular person. It is merely called isalukazana; it is not known who the isalukazana is.

Kepa lezo 'zalukazana kubantu abamnyama zi ya zondeka; a zi fani netongo eli inyoka; ngokuba lapa be bona isalukazana, ba ya *hl*upeka ngokwazi ukuba isalukazana si 'muva-mubi,—umuva waso a u mu*hl*e. Ku ti ku nga vela sona, ku be kona umku*hl*ane omningi pakati kwomuzi, u vame ukututa abantu. Ku be se ku tiwa umuva wesalukazana lowo; noma umuntu wa gwazwa impi, ku be ku ke kwa bonwa isalukazana end*hl*ini yakwake. Ku be se ku tshiwo njalo, ku tiwa umuva waso.

But these lizards are hateful to black men; they are not like the Itongo which is a snake; for when they see an isalukazana, they are troubled because they know that it is an omen of future evil,—that evil comes in its train. Perhaps it appears, and then much fever occurs in the village, which carries off many people. And that is said to be in the train of the isalukazana; or a man is stabbed in battle, after an isalukazana has been seen in his house. And so that too is said to be something which has come in the train of the isalukazana.

Kepa ku te uba nati si i zwe leyo 'ndaba, si kule ng' ezwa umamemkulu, o zala ubaba, e kuluma ngazo izalukazana, lapa mina ngi zi tshaya esibayeni ngamatshe.

But we heard this tale from our grandmother, our father's mother; she told us about these lizards when I killed some in the cattle-pen with stones. For they are

Ngokuba izilwanyana ezi tanda kakulu izigcagi ngenkati yobusika. Ku ti ukupuma kwelanga u si fumane si te ne otini ukunamatela, s' ota ilanga. Ngaloko ke uku si bulala kwami nga m tshela ukulu, nga ti, "Ngi bulele lapa esibayeni izibankhwana ezi ihhambana." Ukulu a ngi tetise ngokuti, "Izalukazana lezo abaninimuzi; a zi bulawa; zi y' esatshwa." Kepa si bone ku isilwane nje isibili sasen*h*le; si goduswe ngemilomo ukuletwa ekaya. Kepa a ku banga 'kcala ngesikati soku zi bulala kwami; kepa amadoda, lapa be zi bona, ba *h*lale se be bheke indaba e za 'uvela.

animals which are very fond of the sunshine during winter. When the sun rises you can find them sticking to a post, basking in the sun. So then when I killed them I told grandmother, saying, "I have killed some little rough lizards in the cattle-pen." Grandmother reproved me, saying, "Those lizards are chiefs of the village; they are not killed; they are reverenced." But we saw it was a mere wild animal; it became domestic from being called an Itongo by the people. But no evil consequences arose when I killed them; but when the men saw them, they constantly looked out for some evil to arise.

Ku ti uma zi bonwa futifuti, ku vele isifo, ku *h*latshwe nenkomo uma i kona, ku tiwe, "A zi d*h*le, zi goduke. Zi funa ni ekaya lapa na? Ini ukuba zi be impi yokubulala umuzi? A zi goduke. Naku ukud*h*la kwenu. Yid*h*la ni, ni hambe." Kepa noma ku tshiwo njalo, a zi muki; ku se si zi bona lapa zi be zi kona izolo. Kodwa abadala a b' esabi ngemva kwokukcola, ngokuba ba ti, "A si se nakcala, loku se si kcolile."

If they are frequently seen, and disease arises, a bullock is sacrificed if there is one, and the people say, "Eat, and go home. What do you want here? Why are you an enemy come to destroy the village? Go home. Here is food for you. Eat and depart." But though they say thus, they do not depart; on the following day we still see them where they were the day before. But the old people are not afraid afterwards, for they say, "We are no longer guilty of aught, for we have paid a ransom."

Crying at the Holes from which Medicines have been dug.

Isimo sabantu abamnyama aba izinyanga, lapa inyanga i mba umuti, i mba i bonga itongo kona lapo, ukuti, "Nansi inkomo, nina 'bakwiti. Lo 'muti ngi u mba nje, ngi temba nina, ukuba ni u nike amand*h*la, u kipe ukufa kulo 'muntu o gulayo, ukuze ngi nconywe ezizweni ukuba ngi inyanga ngani, 'bakwiti."

It is a custom with black doctors, for a doctor when digging up medicines, to dig worshipping the Itongo at the place where he is digging; he says, "Here is a bullock I may gain, ye people of ours. I dig up this medicine trusting in you, that you will give it power to take away the disease from the sick man, that I may become celebrated among the nations, as a great doctor, by your power, ye people of ours."

Ngaloko ke umuti u u mba ngen*h*liziyo em*h*lope, e bheke ukuba ku sinde lowo 'muntu. Kepa uma 'elapile, labo 'bantu ba linga uku mu d*h*la ngobuk*q*ili, nokuti, "O, a si ti kuye, umuti wako nga u d*h*la, a ngi zuzanga 'sikala sokupumula. Kwa ba ngi d*h*le amabele nje." Ngokuba loko kubantu abamnyama ku vamile ukufi*h*la amand*h*la omuti; ba ingcozana aba dumisa imiti. Ngalobo 'buk*q*ili se kwa za kwa funwa izinsaba emakcaleni. Inyanga i ti, "Wena, 'bani, u ye u ngi bekele ind*h*lebe. Nank' umuti wami. Ngi ya 'ku ku vuza. Ngi y' azi ukuba ba ya 'ku u fi*h*la, ba ti, a w enzanga 'luto, b' en*q*ena ukukoka inkomo. Ngaloko ke ngi misa wena, ukuze u ngi bhekele."

He digs up the medicine, then, with a pure heart, expecting the man to get well. But when he has applied his medicines, the people try to eat him up by craft, and say, "Let us tell him that I took his medicine, but gained no relief. It was as though I had taken nothing but corn." For it is common among black men to conceal the power of medicines; they are but few who praise them. In consequence of this craft there came to be appointed secret spies. The doctor says to a man, "So-and-so, do you go and listen for me. There is my medicine. I know that the people will conceal its efficacy, and say it was useless, for they are slow in giving me a bullock. I therefore appoint you to look out for me."

Nembala ke, lapa e s' elapile, a *h*lomele ukuzwa indaba yenkubele yake, ukuti u za 'kuzwa uma se ku njani na. Ku be i loku e tsho njalo, ngokuti, "O, wena kabani, ngi sa gula; a ngi k' ezwa 'ndawo emnandi, nomuti wako lowo kwa ba ngi d*h*le amabele nje." A mangale umniniwo ow aziyo ukwenza kwawo ngapakati kumuntu, 'ezwe umuntu e landula nokukipa ububi ngapakati, a ti, "K*q*a; kwa puma amanzi nje." Kepa in*h*lomeli yake i mu tshele ukuti, "Umuti wako wa sebenza kulo 'muntu; ba ya ku ko*h*lisa; u se hamba emajadwini na sematshwaleni; u se sindile. Kepa inkomo i be lukuni ukupuma; ku kule ukugula kunokupila."

So then when he has treated the patient, he waits to hear what happens, that he may know how he is. And when he hears him say, "O, Son of So-and-so, I am still ill; as yet I am in pain all over; and as to that medicine of yours, it was as if I had only eaten corn." So the owner of the medicine wonders who understands its action in the human body, when he hears the man denying that it even brought any thing away, saying, "No; there came away nothing but water." But his spy tells him that his medicine worked well in the man; that the people deceive him, and the man now goes to wedding-dances and to beer-drinkings; that he is quite well. But it is hard for him to give a bullock; he makes more of the disease which remains than of the health which has been restored.

Inyanga i ze i tsho ukuti, "Bani, loku u ti wena a u yi 'ku ngi nika inkomo, se ngi za 'kuya 'kumbulula amagodi e ng' emba imiti yoku kw elapa kuwo; ngi kale kuwo. Ku kona oku ya 'uvela kuwe, uma nga u ngi d*h*la inkomo yami ngamakcebo. U ze u nga tsho ukuba ngi umtakati. Sa u *h*lala nenkomo leyo. A ngi sa i funi."

At length the doctor says, "So-and-so, since you refuse to give me a bullock, I shall now remember the holes where I dug up the medicine which has cured you; and cry there. Something will happen to you, if you eat my bullock deceitfully. Do not say I am a sorcerer. Keep the bullock. I no longer wish to have it."

Uma nembala e m ko*h*lisa, 'ale, a ti, "O, wena kabani, mina a ngi

If he is really deceiving him, he refuses, saying, "O, Son of So-

tsho ukuba se w a*h*lulekile; ngi ti mina u inyanga yami, noma umuti wako nga u d*h*la, a nga bona 'luto; kepa umzimba ku nga ti u nga ba owomuntu, uma u naka u ngi funel' imiti. Inkomo yako u mina. U ti wena, uma ngi sindile njalo, ngi nga zifi*h*la kanjani na? Musa ukuti u za 'ukala emagodini. Wo ba se u ya ngi bulala uma w enze njalo. Ng' elape nje. Inkomo yako se i kona."

Uma e nga vumelani nenyanga, nembala ke inyanga i vuke ekuseni ngen*h*liziyo ebu*h*lungu kakulu ngokuzwa ngaofakazi ukuba lo 'muntu u m sizile; kep' a nga vumi yena ukuba u siziwe. A ye ke emagodini, e ya 'ku wa panda, e kala izinyembezi, e kuluma ngoku*h*lupeka kwake, e kuluma namatongo akubo, ukuba, "Ku ngani ukuba ni d*h*liwe umuntu, kanti ngi m elape, wa sinda na? A ku bonakale okonakona. Inkomo yami i nge d*h*liwe umuntu o hamba ngezinyawo; a kw a*h*luke imiti yami; a i nga bi ize nje. Ngi kuluma nani nina, kw eyenu. Ng' elapa ngani. Kumnandi ini uma ni d*h*liwa izinkomo na?"

Lapo ke u tsho njalo e kala.

and-so, for my part I do not say the disease has beaten you; I say you are my doctor, although I took your medicine without feeling any effects from it; yet it feels as if my body was about to be that of a man, if you persevere in getting medicines for me. I am your bullock. How do you think, if I get well, I can hide myself? Do not talk about crying at the holes where you dug up the medicines. You will kill me if you do so. Just doctor me. Your bullock is ready for you."

If he does not agree with him, the doctor awakes in the morning with his heart much pained because he hears from witnesses that he has really helped the man; but he will not allow that he has been helped. So he goes to the holes where he dug up the medicines, and scrapes away the earth and sheds tears, and tells the Amatongo of his trouble, saying, "Why are you eaten up by a man whom I have cured? Let the truth appear. Let not my bullock be eaten by a living man; let the power of my medicines be evident, and not be a mere vain thing. I tell you, the medicines were yours. I cured him by your power. Is it pleasant to have your cattle eaten?"

He says this weeping. For it

Ngokuba ku tiwa, amagodi uma e mbululwa ku kalwa, lowo 'muntu ka yi 'kulunga, uma nembala e fi*h*la amand*h*la emiti; u ya 'kufa. Ku njalo ke. Kwiti ku y' esabeka ukuba inyanga i yokala emagodini; ngaloko ku tiwa, ku bang' ukufa loko 'kwenza njalo kwenyanga. I loko ke ukukala emagodini.

is said if the holes where the medicines were dug up be opened, and the doctor weeps there, the man will be ill and die, if he has really concealed the power of the medicines. Thus it is. With us it is a fearful thing that the doctor should go to the holes to cry; and it is said if he does so he calls down death on the patient. This, then, is what is meant by crying at the holes.

Sneezing.

UKUTIMULA kubantu abamnyama ku tiwa ku isibonakaliso sen*h*lan*h*la yokuba umuntu u se nokupila. U ya bonga ngemva kwokutimula, a ti, "Nina 'bakwiti, ukuhamba oku*h*le ngi zuze e ngi ku sweleyo. Ni ngi bheke." Isikati sokutimula isikumbuzo sokuba umuntu a pate itongo lakubo masinyane, ngokuti, "I lona eli ngi pa loku 'kutimula, ukuze ngi li bone ngako ukuba li se nami."

AMONG black men sneezing is said to be a lucky sign that a person will now be restored to health. He returns thanks after sneezing, saying, "Ye people of ours, I have gained that prosperity which I wanted. Continue to look on me with favour." Sneezing reminds a man that he should name the Itongo of his people without delay, because it is the Itongo which causes him to sneeze, that he may perceive by sneezing that the Itongo is with him.

Ku ti uma umuntu e gula e nga timuli, ku ya buzwa ku tiwe ab' ezo'u m bona, "U ke a timule nje na?" be buzela ukuze b' eme isibindi sokuba ukufa loko ku ya 'ubuye ku d*h*lule. Uma e nga timuli ba kunundo ngokuti ukufa kukulu. Ku njalo ke.

If a man is ill and does not sneeze, those who come to see him ask whether he has sneezed or not. They ask that they may take heart and believe that the disease will pass away. If he has not sneezed, they murmur, saying, "The disease is great."

Nengane uma i timula, kuyo ke ku tiwa, "Tutuka!" ku tshiwo ukuhambela pambili en*h*lan*h*leni njalo. Ku isibonakaliso sokupila kwomuntu, nesokupatwa itongo.

Ku njalo ke ukutimula kubantu abamnyama ku vusa amand*h*la okuba umuntu a kumbule ukuba itongo li ngene, li kumina. A bonge ngokutokoza okukulu, e nga ngabazi ngako loko.

Lapa umuntu e ti "Makosi" ekutimuleni, ka tandi ukuti, "Bani wakiti," ngokuba e ng' azi ukuba u mu pi o yena e mu pe loku 'kupila na; ku ngaloko ke u ya *h*langanisa ngokuti, "Makosi, ni nga ngi fulateli." Uma e ti, "Baba," lowo u ya kuluma, kumbe wa timula ngesikati uyise e s' and' ukububa, in*h*liziyo i nga ka ko*h*lwa u ye; u tsho ke ukuti, "Baba, u ngi bheke, ngi be nen*h*lan*h*la kuloko e ngi nge nako."

Noma unina, a tsho njalo, ukuti, "Mame, u nga ngi fulateli." Futi ku tiwa, "Bobaba," e *h*langanisa amatongo akubo onke, abafo baoyise, a se ba fa; a ti, "Bobaba, ni ngi bheke, ni nga ngi fulateli." Noma ku nge si bo aoyisekazi ngesibili, kepa loku se

And if a child sneezes, it is said to it, "Grow!" meaning by this that it should continually advance in prosperity. It is a sign of a man's health, and that the Itongo is with him.

So then sneezing among black men gives a man strength to remember that the Itongo has entered into him and abides with him. And he returns thanks with great joy, having no doubt about it.

When a man, on sneezing, says, "Chiefs," it is because he does not like to say, "So-and-so of our people," because he does not know who it is of the Amatongo who has bestowed on him the benefit; therefore he puts them all together and says, "Chiefs, do not turn your back on me." When he says, "My father," the man who speaks sneezes, perhaps, shortly after his father's death, and his heart does not yet forget him; and so he says, "Father, look upon me, that I may be blessed in such matters as at present I have not."

Or if his mother has lately died he says in like manner, "My mother, do not turn thy back on me." He says, "My fathers," uniting in one all the Amatongo of his people, the brothers of his fathers who are dead; and so he says, "Fathers, look upon me, and do not turn your back on me." And though they may not be in reality his

be file, se be abalondolozi, u ti, "Bobaba," ngaloko.

Amak*x*osa a ti, "Tik*x*o wakowetu, ngi bheke, u be nami njalo, ngi hambe ngen*h*lan*h*la." A kwazeki uma ku nga ka tshiwo ukuti Utik*x*o u yena e itongo lawo Amak*x*osa, a e ti ni na. Manje amakolwa lapa e timula a wa sa tsho ukuti "Baba" etongweni; a se ti, "Mlondolozi, u ngi bheke," noma "Menzi wezulu nom*h*laba." Ku gukqulwe ke njalo loko o be ku kona.

father's brothers, yet since they are dead they are now preservers, and therefore he says, "My fathers."

The Amak*x*osa say, "Utik*x*o of our people, look upon me, and be ever with me, that I may live in prosperity." It is not known what they used to say before they used the word Utik*x*o, who is the Itongo of the Amak*x*osa.[75] And now among the Amak*x*osa believers when they sneeze no longer say to the Itongo "Father," but, "Preserver, look upon me," or, "Creator of heaven and earth." Thus a change has taken place.

UKUTIMULA kubantu abamnyama ba ku biza ngegama lokuti, "Ngi sa pilile. Id*h*lozi li nami; li fikile kumi. A ngi tshetshe ngi bonge kulo, ngokuba i lo eli ti, 'A ngi timule.' Ngemva kwokutimula ngi ya 'kubona iziuto e ngi fanele ukubonga ngazo kwabakwiti, ukuti, 'Nina 'basekutini, e na ti na ti, ngi kcela kuni ukuba ngi zuze izinkomo nabantwana nabafazi, ngi zale kubo, ukuze igama lenu li

WHEN a man among black men sneezes, he says, "I am now blessed. The Idhlozi is with me; it has come to me. Let me hasten and praise it, for it is it which causes me to sneeze. As I have sneezed, I will see the things for which it is proper for me to praise the spirits of the dead belonging to our family, and say, 'Ye of such a place, which did such and such great actions, I ask of you that I may get cattle and children and wives, and have children by them, that your name may not

[75] Utik*x*o is supposed to be a word not originally used by the nations who speak the alliterative class of language; but to be derived from the Hottentot Tikqwa. It is now, however, used by the Amak*x*osa generally, whether Christian or not. But it is not known when the word was first introduced among them, or what have been the causes of its being universally adopted.

nga siteki; ku *h*lale ku tiwe, U kwabani lapaya. Ngokuba uma ngi nge nanzalo, a ku yi 'kutshiwo ukuti, U kwabani lapaya. Uma ngi ngedwa, m*h*laumbe ngi ya 'ku*h*lala em*h*labeni; lapa ngi nge nanzalo, ukufa kwami li ya 'kupela igama lami; ni ya 'kuzwa se ni d*h*la izintete; ngokuba ngaleso 'sikati sokufa kwami u ya 'kuba u se u wile umuzi, a ni 'kungena 'ndawo; ni ya 'kufa amakaza ezintabeni. Amanye amad*h*lozi a ya busisa abantu bawo. Nami ngi ti, Ngi pe ni kakulu; ni nga ngi ko*h*li. Ku ini ukuba n' a*h*lulwe i mi, ngi ngedwa na? Uma si ba ningi, nga ku njani na?' "

perish, but it may still be said, That is the village of So-and-so yonder. For if I have no children, it will not be said, That is the village of So-and-so yonder. If I am alone, it may be I shall live long on the earth; if I have no children, at my death my name will come to an end; and you will be in trouble when you have to eat grasshoppers; for at the time of my death my village will come to an end, and you will have no place into which you can enter; you will die[76] of cold on the mountains. Other Amadhlozi bless their people. And I too say, Give me abundantly; do not forget me. Why are you unable to give me, I being alone? If we were many, how would it be?' "

Vows to Sacrifice to the Amatongo.

Uma ku gula umuntu, kepa ku nge ko isikati soku i *h*laba inkomo, ngokuba a ku yiwanga enyangeni, ku tiwa umnini umntwana ematongweni, "Uma ku i nina, 'bakwiti

If a person is ill, and there is not time to sacrifice an ox, for they have not been to a diviner, the father of the child addresses the Amatongo thus:—"If it is you,

[76] He does not speak of the actual death of the Amatongo; for the people believe that the Amatongo do not die, but of their suffering from cold. In another place we read of killing an imamba which was the Itongo of Udingane. Under such circumstances the people say, "I pind' i vuke," It comes to life again. And they say it is the same identical snake which rises to life again, for if it has been killed by any particular wound, it will have the mark of the wound on its body.

ab' enza nje, ngi beka; nansi inkomo etile; ka sinde Ubani, ni i d*h*le." Noma e nga tsho "ukubeka" kakulu, a ti, "Ngi misa inkomo; nansi; ka sinde." Uma i nge ko inkomo, u ya kala uyise ngokuti, "Po, uma ni funa inyama, ku njani ukuba ni nga m pilisi, ngi hambe ngi i tate inkomo na, ngi ni *h*labele, ni d*h*le? Ngi ya 'kubona kanjani uma e nga vuki na ukuba i nina?" A nga tsho ukuti, "Ngi ni misela ukuya 'kulanda inkomo," ukuti ke, "Ngi linde ni; ngi ya 'ku ni funela, ngi fike nenkomo yenu."

people of our house, who are doing this, I make a vow; behold there is such and such a bullock; let the child get well, that you may eat." Or he may not say "devote," but, "I set apart a bullock; there it is. Let the child get well." Or if he does not possess a bullock, the father cries, saying, "If you wish for food, why do you not cure my child, that I may go and get you a bullock, and kill it for you, that you may eat? How shall I know that it is you, if the child does not get well?" Or he may say, "I vow to you to go and fetch you a bullock," that is, "Wait for me; I am going to find you a bullock, and will bring it home for you."

It may be worth while to note the curious coincidence of thought among the Amazulu regarding the Amatongo or Abapansi, and that of the Scotch and Irish regarding the fairies or "good people."

For instance, the "good people" of the Irish have ascribed to them in many respects the same motives and actions as the Amatongo. They call the living to join them, that is, by death; they cause disease which common doctors cannot understand, nor cure; they have their feelings, interests, partialities, and antipathies, and contend with each other about the living. The common people call them their friends or people, which is equivalent to the term *abakubo* given to the Amatongo. They reveal themselves in the form of the dead, and it appears to be supposed that the dead become "good people," as the dead among the Amazulu become Amatongo: and in the funeral processions of the "good people," which some have professed to see, are recognised the forms of those who have just died; as Umkatshana saw his relatives among the Abapansi.[77] And the power of holding communion with the "good people" is consequent on an illness, just as the power to divine among the natives of this country.[78]

So also in the Highland Tales, a boy who had been carried away by the fairies, on his return to his home speaks of them as "our folks," which is equivalent to *abakwetu*, applied to the Amatongo.[79] And among the Highlanders they are called "the good people," "the folk." They are also said to "live underground," and are therefore Abapansi, or Subterraneans.[80]

They are also, like the Abapansi, called ancestors. Thus "the Red Book of Clanrannald is said not to have been dug up, but to have been found *on* the moss. It seemed as if the ancestors sent it."[81]

---

77 See Nursery Tales of the Zulus, p. 317.

78 See Croker's Fairy Legends, especially "The Confessions of Tom Bourke," p. 46.

79 Campbell. Vol. II., p. 56.

80 Id., p. 65, 66.

81 Id., Vol. II., p. 106.

DREAMS, &c.

DREAMS, subjective apparitions, and similar psychical phenomena are in the native mind so intimately wrapped up with the Amatongo, that this is the proper place for considering their views on such matters, without which their views on the Amatongo would be incomplete.

The Amatongo make revelations by Dreams.

UMA u lele wa pupa umuntu o nga m azelele ukuba a nga kw enza kabi; kepa ku ti ebusuku u lele, u bone e ku gwaza ngoku ku zuma, e nga ku gwazi obala, e ku d*h*la imfi*h*lo, uma se u vuka, u ya mangala kakulu, u ti, "Wau! Kanti Ubani lo, ngi ti, umuntu omu*h*le nje, kanti u ya ngi zonda na?" U ti, "Ngi ya li bonga itongo lakwiti eli veze lo 'muntu kumina, ngi nga m azi. Manje ngi nga m azi, loku itongo se li m fikisile. Wa fika e ngi bulala, ngi nga lw azi uluto lwake e ngi lu d*h*lile." U *h*lale, u m *h*lakanipile lowo 'muntu ngokuti, "Leli 'pupo a li tsho 'manga; i kona indaba e ngi nga y aziyo, e kulo 'muntu."

IF during sleep you dream of a man whom you do not thoroughly know to be of such a character that he may do you an injury; yet if in your sleep you dream that he suddenly stabs you, not openly, but by stealth, when you awake you are much amazed and say, "Oh! Forsooth I thought such a one a really good man. And does he hate me? I thank the Itongo of our people which has revealed the man to me, that I may know him. Now I know him, for the Itongo has caused him to approach me. And he came to kill me. I do not know in what respect I have injured him." And you continue on your guard against the man, believing that the dream does not lie, but that there is something in the man with which you are not acquainted.

Futi uma u lele u pupe isilwane si ku zingela, si funa uku ku bulala, ku ti uma u vuke, u mangale u ti, "Hau! Ku njani loku, uma ngi pupe isilo si ngi zingela?" Ku ti uma ku ya 'uzingelwa kusasa,

Again, if in your sleep you dream of a beast pursuing you and trying to kill you, when you wake you wonder and say, "How is this that I should dream of a wild beast pursuing me?" And if in the morning they are going to

noma izilo noma izinyamazane, u hambe w azi ukuba "Ngi sengozini;" w azi ukuba "Lesi 'silo si letwe itongo, ukuze ng' azi ukuba uma ngi nga bheki, ngi nga fa." Uma u ya enk*q*ineni, u ye se u *h*lakanipile. Kumbe u nga yi, ngokuti, "Isalakutshelwa si zwa ngomopo." U ti, "A ngi *h*lale." U *h*lale, u zilondolozile, ngokuti, "Ngi sa funa kupi, loku itongo se li ngi tshelile, ukuba ngi ya empini?"

Futi, uma u lele ubutongo, u pupe u buyela kwabakini, uma w' a*h*lukana nabo isikati se si side; u bone be *h*lezi kabi, aobani naobani; u vuka umzimba u mude; w azi ukuba "Itongo eli ngi yise kulabo bakwiti, ukuze ngi bone lobo 'bubi a ba nabo; uma ngi ya kona, i kona indaba e ngi nga i fumana kona yoku*h*lala kabi." U *h*lale u beke ind*h*lebe, u *h*lomele ukuti, "Ngi ya 'kuzwa indaba, uma ku kona umuntu." Nembala ku ti ku nga fika umuntu wangakona, u buze in*h*lalo yabakini. Uma e ku tshela uku*h*lala kubi, u

hunt, whether wild beasts or game, you go knowing that you are in jeopardy; you know that the Itongo brought the beast to you, that you might know that if you do not take care you may die. If you go to the hunt, you are on your guard. Perhaps you do not go, saying, "Isalakutshelwa hears through trouble.[82] Let me stay at home." And you stay at home and take care of yourself, saying, "What do I want further, when the Itongo has already told me that I am going into danger?"[83]

Again, if during sleep you dream of returning to your people from whom you separated a long time ago; and see that So-and-so and So-and-so are unhappy; and when you wake your body is unstrung;[84] you know that the Itongo has taken you to your people that you might see the trouble in which they are; and that if you go to them you will find out the cause of their unhappiness. And you continue listening and expecting to hear news if any one comes. And truly a man may come from the neighbourhood, and you ask after the welfare of your people. If he tells you they are in bad circumstances, you say, "O, I mere-

[82] *Is'-ala-'kutshelwa*, He who when told refuses to listen, hears in the time of trouble. A proverbial saying. Another form is, *Ihlonga-'ndhlebe li zwa ngomopo*, He who is without an ear hears in the time of trouble.

[83] *Empini*, lit., to an army, or enemy.

[84] *Umzimba u mude*, your body is long, that is, relaxed, unstrung.

ti, "O, ngi buza kodwa. Se ng' ezwa ngepupo." Futi, uma umuntu e file, kanti ku kona o m *h*lekako ngaloko 'kufa, e nga m kaleli, noma e se file u ya buya a buze komunye o sa pilile, a ti, "Ubani lo u ngi *h*leka ngokufa, ngokuba yena e nga yi 'kufa ini na?" Kw aziwe ngepupo ukuba Ubani lo kanti u ya *h*leka. Ku tiwe leli 'zwi li fike nesitunzi sake o fileko.

Futi, kubantu abamnyama, ku ti ngesikati sokuvama kwempi, abantu abaningi ba sinde itongo; li fika ngepupo; kumbe pakati kwobusuku umuntu a pupe e vuswa Ubani, umuntu wakubo owa fako; a ti, "Bani, vuka, u tate abantwana bako nezinkomo, u pume. I ya ngena impi lapa." Ku ti ngokudelela, e ti, "Ipupo nje," a lale. Li pinde li fike li ti, "Vuka." Ubutongo bu ze bu be bubi. A k*q*ale ukubona ukuba indaba le. Kumbe a t' e ti sululu, i be i vimbezela, 'ezwe se ku kala abantu. A bonge kakulu itongo lakubo.

Ukufika kwalo 'muntu ka fiki e inyoka, nesitunzi nje; ku fike

ly ask. I have already heard the news in my dream." And if one dies, and there is one who laughs at his death and does not mourn for him, and if the dead man return again and enquire of another who is still living, saying, "Does So-and-so laugh at my death because he will not die?" it is known by the dream that the other laughs. It is said the shade of the dead comes with the message.

Further, among black men, when enemies are numerous, many people are saved by the Itongo; it comes in a dream; perhaps in the middle of the night a man dreams that one of his people who is dead wakes him, saying, "So-and-so, awake, and take your children and cattle, and go away. An enemy is coming into this village." And through despising it and thinking it a mere dream, he goes to sleep. And the Itongo comes again and says, "Awake." And at length he cannot sleep well. And he begins to see there is something real in the dream. Perhaps just as he has got out of the way the enemy surrounds the village, and he hears the people crying. He then returns hearty thanks to the Itongo of his people.

When a dead man comes he does not come in the form of a

yena ukqobo lwako nje, ngokungati ka fanga, a kulume nomuntu wakubo; na lowo e nga tsho ukuti umuntu owa fayo, a ze a bone uma e se papama ukuti, "Kanti ngi ti Ubani u sa hamba nje; kanti ku fike isitunzi sake." Ku ti uma wa fa izinto zake zi semzimbeni nokubuya u buya e se nazo; lezo 'zinto z' aziwa.

snake, nor as a mere shade; but he comes in very person, just as if he was not dead, and talks with the man of his tribe; and he does not think it is the dead man until he sees on awaking, and says, "Truly I thought that So-and-so was still living; and forsooth it is his shade which has come to me." And when he returns he has the same clothes on as those in which he died, and the clothes are known.

Futi ku kona kwabamnyama inyoka i ngena end*h*lini; i bonwe, ku bizwane, ku tiwe, "Nansi inyoka." Abantu ba ti budubudu ukuya 'u i bona leyo 'nyoka, uma i nga baleki. Ba ti, "Uma eyasend*h*le, nga i baleka i bona abantu. Kepa loku a i baleki, eyasekaya." Abanye ba ti, "Isilwane; a i bulawe." Ku pikiswane; omunye a i bulale, i la*h*lwe ngapand*h*le. Ku lalwe. Ipupo li fike; lo 'muntu owa fayo, li ti, "Ku ngani ukuba ni ngi bulale, ni ngi bona na? U mina lowo e ni m bulele. Ngi Ubani." A vuke lowo 'muntu, a wa lauze lawo 'mapupo. Ku mangalwe. Ku ngaloko ke ku tiwa inyoka i itongo. Ku tshiwo ngokuba ku tsho wona e ti, "U mina leyo 'nyoka e ni i bonileko."

Sometimes among black men a snake enters the house; when it is seen they call one another, saying, "There is a snake." All the people hurry to look at the snake if it does not run away. They say if it were a wild snake[85] it would run away when it sees men. But as it does not run away, it is a tame snake.[86] Others say, "It is a beast; let it be killed." They dispute, and one kills it and throws it away. They go to sleep, and a dream comes, and the dead man says, "How is it that you kill me when you see me? It is me whom you have killed. I am So-and-so." The man awakes, and tells his dreams, and the people wonder. It is on this account, then, that they say that the Itongo is a snake. They say so because the dead man tells them in dreams that he is the snake which they have seen.

85 *Eyasendhle*, a wild snake, that is, not an Itongo.
86 *Eyasekaya*, a home snake, that is, an Itongo.

Ecstasy and Dreams.

Isiyezi si njengokuba umuntu wa fa kancinyane. U ya vuka u se bona izinto a nga zi boni uma e nge nasiyezi.

Undayeni umuntu o be *h*lakanipile o be tsho ukuti, "Ngi namand*h*la okubona oku ngalapaya," noko e nge ko lapo. U ya ku bona ngesinye isikati oku ngalapaya, a tsho kubantu ukuti, "U kona umuntu, u y' eza ngale 'nd*h*lela," noma isi*h*lobo sake, noma umuntu nje.

Ngesinye isikati ezweni lakwiti ku be ku zingelwa izinyati. Uma e lele ebusuku, u ya 'kuvuka kusasa, a si tshele, a ti, "Madoda, uma si ya 'kuzingela izinyati nam*h*la nje, i kona into en*h*le e ya 'kuvela ekuhambeni kwetu. Ngi fumene izinyati ebusuku, si zi zingela; za ba izinkomo nje." Li pela lapo lelo 'pupo eli njalo. Izinyati si fike kuzo, zi be njengezinkomo njalo njengokutsho kwake; si zi bulale, si nga bi namdwa nomuncinyane nje.

Ngesinye ke isikati, uma ku kona ukuzingela, abantu be be *h*langene ngokuti, "Madoda, ngosuku olutile ku fanele ukuba ke si yozingela izinyati emfuleni otile."

Ecstasy is a state in which a man becomes slightly insensible. He is awake, but still sees things, which he would not see if he were not in a state of ecstasy.

Undayeni was a clever man, who used to say he was able to see things afar off from him. He would sometimes see what was going on on the other side of a hill, and tell the people, saying, "There is a man coming by that path," whether it was a friend, or a stranger.[87]

Sometimes in our country they hunted buffalo. If he had slept at night, he would awake in the morning and tell us, saying, "Sirs, if we go to hunt buffaloes to-day, we shall be lucky. I saw some buffaloes during the night; we were hunting them; they were just like cattle." That was all such dreams made known to us. When we found the buffaloes, they were just like cattle, as he had told us; we killed them, and did not get so much as a scratch.

On another occasion, if there was a hunt, the men having already agreed, saying, "Sirs, on such a day it is well for us to go and hunt buffaloes by such a river."

---

87 That is, in the ecstatic state he could see that some one was coming, but could not see whether it was an acquaintance, or a stranger.

Ba vumelane. Ku se kusasa ba puma, ba hamba. Ku ti ekuhambeni a tsho, a ti, "Madoda, kodwa ngi bonile ekulaleni kwami, noko si ya 'uzingela, a no zingela ngobudoda. Izinyati, ngi ti, zi nolaka." Mbala, ku be njalo eku zi fumaneni kwabo; noma zi nga bulalanga 'muntu, zi vame uku ba ponsa noma izinja. Ba ya ya kuzo se be *h*lakanipile ngokupupa kwake; ba ya 'kuvika futifuti.

They would agree, and when the morning arrived set out on their journey. As they were setting out he would say to them, "Sirs, but I have seen in my sleep, although we are going to hunt, do you hunt like men. For I say the buffaloes are full of rage." And truly it was so when they came up with them; although they did not kill any one, they tossed the men or dogs continually. But they went to the hunt made cautious by his dream; and escaped again and again by dodging.

Sa m bona ukuti, noko e nge si inyanga, kodwa ukupupa kwake ku*h*le. Futi wa e indoda e kalipayo, e nesibindi; uma inyati i ya 'kumisa obala, lapo ku nge ko 'muti wokukwela umuntu, yena a ti, "Kwela ni emitini nina. Ngi za 'kuya, ngi ye 'kuyoka ukuze i ze kunina, si i bulale." Kodwa abantu b' a*h*luleke, ukuti, "U za 'kuyoka e nga hambi pezulu, e nge najubane nje? U ya 'kwenza njani na? U ya 'kubaleka kanjani na?" Noko a hambe a ye kuyo, a i k*q*ale ngomkonto, a i *h*labe, a baleke a ye kona lapo be kona abantu, a kwele emtini; uma ku kona abantu aba nemikonto, ba i *h*labe, i ze i fe.

We noticed that although he was not an inyanga, yet his dreams were good. He was besides a brave man and courageous; if there were a buffalo in an open spot, where was no tree upon which a man could climb, he would say to the people, "Do you climb into the trees. I will go and draw him towards you, that we may kill him." But the people could not see that, but said, "How will he draw the buffalo towards us, for he cannot fly, and is not able to run fast? What will he do? How will he escape?" But he went to the buffalo, and began the attack by stabbing it, and then ran away to where the people were, and climbed into a tree; and if there were any men who had assagais, they killed it.

Abantu ba be ti ngaye, u inyanga, noko e nga buli; u tsho okubonakalayo; ngokuba izinyanga, noko zi bula, ngesinye isikati zi tsho okungabonakaliyo. Wa e intwesi futi yamazwi, ngokuba amazwi ake a e bonakala.

The people used to say of him, that he was a diviner though he did not divine; for he said what was true; and diviners sometimes say what is not true. He was also an eloquent man, for what he said came to pass.

Kwa tiwa, amad*h*lozi akubo nakoninalume—akoninalume a tanda uku m enza inyanga, akubo a wa tandanga. Ngemva kwaloko ka be sa ba nako ukubula njengezinyanga; kodwa yena wa kuluma nje ngomlomo, ka bula. Kodwa ukwenza kwake kwa ku fana nenyanga, e nge si yo noko; ngokuba u be e zamula futifuti, a timule njalonjalo; loko ke okwezinyanga ezi bulayo; noko e nga buli, wa e pakati kwaleyo 'ndawo yokubula nokungabuli.

It was said, the Amatongo of his own people and the Amatongo of his maternal uncle disagreed. Those of the maternal uncle wished to make him a diviner; those of his own people did not wish it. After that he was unable to divine like a diviner; but said what was true without divination. But his habits were those of a diviner, though he was not one; for he used to yawn and sneeze continually; and this is done by diviners; although he did not divine, he was midway between divining and not divining.

Indaba e ngi i kumbulayo enye kandayeni. Kwa ti si s' ake emgeni; kwa ku kona idwala li nengobozi, lapo ku ma amanzi kona; kepa sonke tina si 'batsha lawo 'manzi e isibuko setu, lapo si zibuka kona. Ku te ngolunye usuku wa si buza, e vuka ebutongweni, wa ti, "I kona ini indawo edwaleni, lapo ni zibuka kona na?" Sa ti, "Ku kona ni kona na?" Wa ti, "Ai. Ngi ya buza, ngo-

There is another thing which I remember of Undayeni. We were living on the Umgeni; there was in the neighbourhood a rock, in which was a hollow, where water stood; and that water was the looking glass in which all we younger ones used to look at ourselves. One day on awaking from sleep he asked us, saying, "Is there a place in the rock which you gaze in as a looking glass?" We replied, "What harm is there in that?" He replied, "No. I merely ask because I have seen

kuba ngi bonile e ngi ku bonileyo ebusuku." Sa vuma, sa ti, "I kona." Wa ti, "Ngi ti, kuleyo 'ndawo ni nga be ni sa ya kona. U kona umuntu o kade e ni bona ukuba se n' ejwayele kuleyo 'ndawo ukuzibuka. Kepa u fake ububi kuleyo 'ndawo. I yeke ni leyo 'ndawo." Kepa ngokuba nembala kwa ku umuntu e si m azi, ukuti u kuluma isiminya, a si pikanga, sa vuma, sa i yeka leyo 'ndawo. Loko ke ka ku bonanga esiyezini, wa ku bona e lele.

Ngokuba na sendabeni, uma ku kona umuntu o nekcala, kepa Undayeni uma e ti, "Bani, indaba i ya 'ku ku lahla." Nembala lowo 'muntu, uma e m azi, a ku sa swelekile kuye ukuba a ye emakcaleni; u se e fanele ukuti a zilungisele kahle kulo 'muntu, ku nga yiwa emakcaleni.

U be njalo ke ukuhamba kwake. I loko ke e ngi ku kumbulayo ukwenza kwake.

Kepa ngesiyezi a be e bona ngaso, u be umuntu kakulu o nga tandi ukuhlala pakati kweningi labantu; u be tanda ukuzihlalela yedwa, ngokuba u be umuntu kakulu e si ti u kuluma isiminya.

what I have seen during the night." Then we told him that there was such a place. He replied, "I tell you never to go to that place again. There is some one who for some time has seen that you are accustomed to look at yourselves there. And he has put bad medicine[88] into the hollow. Leave the place." And because he was a man whom we knew, we saw that he spoke the truth, and did not refuse to obey, but left the place. This he did not see in an ecstatic state, but during sleep.

And even in disputes, if there was any one who was in fault, and Undayeni said to him, "So-and-so, you will lose the case,"—if the man knew Undayeni he would no longer want to go into court, but was now ready to act rightly to the other without going into court.

Such then was the character of Undayeni. This is what I remember of his acts.

And as regards the ecstasy into which he fell, he was a man who did not like to sit in the midst of many people; but liked to sit alone, for he was a man who, we said, spoke the truth.[89] I do not

[88] *Ububi*, that is, some medicinal substance, capable of making any one who looked into the water hateful to others. See "Superstitious Use of Medicines."—Among the Highland Tales there is mentioned a magic basin which made a person beautiful when he washed in it. (*Campbell. Vol. I., p.* 97.)

[89] He sat alone that he might become ecstatic, and in that state see what he could not see in his ordinary condition.

A ngi tsho ukuti u be nga *h*lali nakanye pakati kwabantu, kodwa u be nga vami.

Njengaloku pakati kwabantu abamnyama indaba zamapupo ku tiwa a y aziwa ukuma kwawo. Ngokuba amanye amapupo a ya vela njengokungati ku njalo, kanti a ku njalo; amanye a kombise indaba e za 'kwenzeka. Ngokuba ku kona pakati kwabantu abamnyama ukuti, uma umuntu e lele wa bona iketo elikulu, ku sinwa; uma ku gula umuntu, a ku tshiwo ukuti si y' etemba ukuti u ya 'kusinda; masinyane kulowo 'muntu o bone ku sinwa, u y' esaba kakulu, a *h*lale e se beka ind*h*lebe; uma ku umuntu o nge si ye walapo ku gulwayo, e beka ind*h*lebe, ngokuti u za 'kuzwa isililo. Kepa noma ku nge si yo leyo 'mini ukuba ku kalwe, ku y' esabeka, a ku tembeki loko 'kupupa.

Kepa ukupupa okutembekayo kubantu abamnyama, uma umuntu o gulayo ku putshwe e se e file, e se e ya 'kula*h*lwa egodini, ba bone nokug*q*itshwa kwake, nokukalelwa kwake konke, nokula*h*lwa kwezinto zake ku pele ngaleso 'sikati sobusuku. Ku tiwa ke ngaloko, "Ngokuba si m pupela ukufa, ka yi 'kufa."

mean that he never sat amidst other people, but he did not usually do so.

In like manner among black men the real meaning of dreams is not known. For some dreams have every appearance of reality, but they are not true; others point out something which is about to happen. For among black men it is supposed that if a man dream of a great assembly, where they are dancing, if there is any one ill, we have no confidence that he will get well; but immediately the man who dreamt of the dance is much alarmed, and if he is not a man of the same village as that where the man is ill, he continually listens, expecting to hear the funeral wail. And although the wail is not heard on the same day, he is still fearful and without confidence.

But a dream which produces confidence among black men, when any one is ill, is one in which they dream that someone is dead and about to be buried, and that they see the earth poured into the grave, and hear the funeral lamentation for him, and see the destruction[90] of all his things during the night. They say of such a dream, "Because we have dreamt of his death he will not die."

[90] Some of the dead man's personal property—as his assagais, his blanket, and dress—is buried with him, and some is burnt.

A s' azi ke uma loko kw enza ngani. Lokupela njengokuma kwokupila nokufa ku be ku fanele ukuba o za 'kufa nembala a fe, uma e gula e putshwa; a ti o za 'kupila a pile, uma ku putshwa e pila. Nembala loko ngi ku bonile kokobili. Ijadu ngi li bonile, umuntu wa fa; futi ukufa ngi ku bonile ngomuntu o be gula, kepa wa pila. Njengokuba ekuguleni kwomfundisi wetu ngonyaka owa d*h*lulayo, nga m pupa e se e file, e fele emgungund*h*lovu. Kepa ka la*h*lwanga emalibeni, wa la*h*lwa pakati kwend*h*lu em*h*lope ngapakati; kepa ku gcwele abantu abaningi abafayo, e se lele ngapezulu kwalabo 'bantu; ikanda lake li bheke empumalanga, izinwele zi fi*h*le ame*h*lo. Loko nga ku bona ngi lele. Ekuvukeni kwami a ngi *h*lalelanga, ukuti, "A ngi bheke ukuba nembala incwadi e za 'kufika; i za 'kufika, i ti, 'O, se ku njalo, u file.'" A ngi *h*lalelanga loko; nga vuka nje, nga bona se ku njalo; nga kala masinyane ngabo lobo 'busuku; ng' esaba nokuba incwadi i fike, ngokuti i za 'kutsho loko. Kwa nga i ng' epuza ukufika. Nga *h*lala ngi zije-

We do not understand how this happens. For as regards living and dying, it would appear proper that he who is about to die should die, if when he is ill people dream he is dead; and he who is is about to live should live, if people dream that he is well. But in truth I have seen both. I have dreamt of a wedding-dance, and the man died; again, I have dreamt of the death of a sick man, but he got well. For example, when some years ago our Teacher was ill, I dreamt that he was dead, and that he had died at Pietermaritzburg. But he was not buried in a grave, but was placed in the middle of a house which was white inside; and it was full of dead men, and he was placed on the top of the dead men; his head was directed towards the east, and his hair covered his eyes. This I saw in my sleep. When I awoke, I waited, saying, "Let me look out for the letter which will come shortly; it will come and say, 'O, it is so, he is dead.'" I did not wait for that, but saw it was already really true, and at once wept during the rest of the night; I was afraid for a letter to come, thinking it would tell us of his death. I longed that it might be a long time before it arrived. My eyes remained full of tears

jana ngaloko 'kupupa. Kepa ekufikeni kwencwadi a kwa ba njalo. Ng'ezwa ilizwi lokuti, "U ti, a ku kupuke inqola, u m *hl*angabeze." Nga ti, "O, nembala ukupupa ukufa a ku bonisisi ukufa."

A ngi ka kqedi ukuti se ku isiminya loko; ngokuba kwabanye ba bona ukufa, nembala ku be i ko; nokupila ngesinye isikati ku be ukupila. Kepa nami a ngi tsho ukuti ukupupa ku hamba ngaloko oku bonwayo umuntu; ngesinye isikati ngi nga pupa into, nembala i ya 'kuba njalo njengokuba ngi i bonile. Kepa kakulu ngi ya kuluma ngokufa kwomuntu ogulayo nokupila, ukuti, a ku hambi ngend*hl*ela e be ku fanele ukuhamba ngayo; ku ya pambanisa.

Abantu ba ti, amapupo ase*hl*obo a tsho isiminya; kepa a ba tsho ukuti, a tsho isiminya kanyekanye; kodwa ba ti, e*hl*obo a ku vamile ukuba amapupo a geje. Kodwa ba ti, ubusika bubi, bu fika namaongoongo, ukuti, amapupo amaningi kakulu a nga kqondekiyo ka*hl*e. Kepa ngaloko a ku tshiwo ukuti, ubusika bu pupisa ka*hl*e, noma umuntu e pupile amapupo, uma e wa lauzela omunye, lowo u ti masinyane, "O, 'bani, amaongoongo obusika lawo,"

because of the dream. But when the letter came it was not so. But I heard it said, "Our Teacher has sent for the waggon to go to Pietermaritzburg, to fetch him." So I said, "O, truly, to dream of death does not show that death will take place."

I have not yet come to a certain conclusion that this is true; for some dream of death, and death occurs; and sometimes of health, and the person lives. And I do not say that a dream turns out to be true; sometimes I dream of something, and in fact the thing happens as I have dreamed. But I speak especially of the death or life of one who is ill, that the event turns out different from what it ought to, and goes by contraries.

People say, summer dreams are true; but they do not say they are always true; but they say that summer dreams do not usually miss the mark. But they say the winter is bad, and produces confused imaginations, that is, very many unintelligible dreams. And therefore it is said that winter causes bad dreams, and if a man has dreamed and tells another, he will at once answer him, saying, "O, So-and-so, that is nothing but the confused imaginations caused by the winter." He says thus

e tsho ngokuba e ti, a ku ko 'n*h*lamvu pakati kwawo. Njengaloku i*h*lobo ku tiwa, a li nazo izindaba eziningi zamanga. Kepa uma se ku fike ubusika, abantu ba ya k*q*ala ukuba nevuso, ngokuti, bu za 'kufika ke ubusika namafukufuku amaningi, ukuti amanga.

Ipupo e ku tiwa li vela etongweni, uma li fika ngezwi likabani o nga se ko, ukuti, "Ini uma ku ng' enziwa ukuti nokuti na?" Njengaloku kubantu abamnyama, uma u zuze amabele kakulu, ngesinye isikati ku ti ekulaleni kumninimuzi a pupe, ku tiwa, "Ini ukuba u piwe ukud*h*la okungaka, u nga bongi na?" Kepa masinyane uma e se e vukile ka ngabazi ukuti leli 'pupo li tsho 'kud*h*la kuni? U ya bona nje ukuti, "O, nembala!" A be e se ti emzini wake, "A kw enziwe utshwala; ku ya 'ku*h*latshwa." A be ke e se bonga ngaloko 'kud*h*la a kw enzileyo. Noma e zuze izinkomo, 'enze njalo futi.

Kwa ti ngesikati lapa Amazulu a ya empini, emuva kwaloko kwa *h*latshwa umkosi ukuti, "Zi mi

because there is no sense in the dream. In like manner it is said there is not much that is false in the dreams of summer. But when the winter comes the people begin to be afraid that the winter will bring much rubbish, that is, false dreams.

A dream which is said to be sent by the Itongo, is one which comes with a message from the dead, enquiring why such and such a thing is not done. For example, among black men, if one has an abundant harvest sometimes the head of the village dreams that it is said to him, "How is it, when you have been given so much food, that you do not give thanks?" And as soon as he wakes he has no doubt as to what food the dream means. But he perceives at once that the dream speaks to the point. And he immediately commands his people to make beer, for he is about to sacrifice. So he praises the Amatongo for the food which they have given him. And if he has gained many cattle he does the same.

It happened once when the Amazulu had gone out to battle,[91] the word was passed among the people telling them that the cattle were standing without guard at

[91] To fight with the Dutch in the time of Udingane.

zodwa ed*hl*okweni." Kepa bonke abantu b' esukela pezulu, ukuti b' eza 'utola izinkomo. Kw' esuka namak*x*egu e pete izindondolo; kepa lolo 'lusinga olu njalo lwa za lwa susa nobaba. Lokupela ya fika ntambama leyo 'ndaba, wa ti komame, "Ngi gayele ni isinkwa, ngi ze ngi d*hl*e end*hl*eleni." Kepa ekulaleni kwake, kwa fika ilizwi, la ti, "U nga yi lapo ku yiwako; a ku yi 'kubuya namunye." Nembala ekuseni, ngokuba kwa ku i*hl*azo uma indoda i ti, "Mina a ngi yi," kepa wa ti, "O, mina, 'bakwiti, ngi lele ngi zilungisele ukuhamba; kepa manje ku se umlenze wami w ala; se ngi ya k*x*uga." Nembala wa zik*x*ugisa.

Idhlokwe.[92] And all the people started up, thinking they should get cattle; and even old men went out, leaning on their staves; and at length our father was carried away by the infection. And as the news came in the afternoon, he said to our mothers, "Make me some bread, that I may eat on the journey." But whilst he was asleep a voice came to him, saying, "Do not go where the others are going; not one will come back again." So in the morning, as it was a shame to a man to say he was not going, he said, "O, for my part, neighbours, when I lay down I had got ready to go; but now my leg prevents me; I have become lame." In fact he pretended to be lame.

Ba hamba be ti, ba za 'kutitiliza; kanti ukufa ku ya 'kutitiliza bona. O, kwa fika wa ba munye, Usihhile; e fika, be m dabule ikanda ek*c*aleni kwend*hl*ebe ngomkonto; e ti, "Ni bona mina nje ukupela." Loko kwa k*q*iniseka kubaba, ukuti, "Nembala ngi vusiwe ngepupo." Kepa wa li lauza lelo 'pupo emveni ukuti, "Nami be ngi ya, kepa ngi bone loko ebusuku."

They set out thinking they should gain very many cattle; and forsooth death made a very great gain of them. O, one only came back, whose name was Usichile; he came with an assagai wound by his ear. He said, "You see me only." That was a confirmation to my father that he had been truly warned by the dream. And after that he told the dream, saying, "I too was going, but I saw what has happened in a dream."

---

[92] *Id*hl*okwe*, a secure place, where there was abundant pasture and forest, where the cattle could feed in concealment.

Futi ngepupo uma ku *h*laselwa, umuntu wa lala, wa pupa e gwaza umuntu kuk*q*ala, a m bulale, ekuvukeni kwake u y' enyela ngokuti, "Hau! ku njani loku, uma ngi pupe ngi bulala umuntu? K*q*a. La 'mapupo a ya pambanisa. Ku ya 'kufa mina." A hambe ngoku*h*lakanipa—a nga hambi pambili, a hambe emuva; i *h*langane k*q*ede, anduba a ngene, impi se i 'me*h*lo 'mnyama, a gwaze umuntu. A nga ko*h*lwa i lelo 'pupo, a zing' e l' azi njalo.

UMPENGULA MBANDA.

Again, if when making an incursion into another country one has dreamt that he stabbed a man first and killed him, he murmurs saying, "Oh, how is it that I have dreamt that I killed a man? No. The dream goes by contraries. It is I who shall be killed." So he goes cautiously—does not go in front, but behind the others; but when the two armies have joined battle, then he enters into the engagement, when the enemy is confused, and stabs someone. He does not forget the dream, but bears it constantly in mind.

Uguaise's Dream.

INHLIZIYO yami imbi. Ngi kwel' o[93] ubutongo obubi. Nga pupa isililo, ku kala abantu be baningi. Ya ba mbi in*h*liziyo yami, ngokuba ngi pupe izinto eziningi! Nga pupa nomjadu, abantu abaningi abasinayo.

In*h*liziyo yami ya kcabanga ukuba umjadu u ipupo elibi. Uma u pupa umjadu, ku ba ka ku lungile; ku ba u kona umuntu ofileyo; umjadu u isililo; uma u pupa abantu be sina, libi lelo 'pupo.

MY heart is heavy. I have had a bad dream. I dreamt of a funeral lamentation; many people were weeping. How heavy my heart is because I have dreamt of many things! I dreamt also of a wedding-dance; many people were dancing.

I thought in my heart, a wedding is a bad dream. If you dream of a wedding, there is something not right; there is someone who has died; the wedding is a sign of lamentation; if you dream of men dancing, it is a bad dream.

---

[93] A similar form of expression occurs in the following sentence —Nga se ngi zwa isililo, se ku kalwa ukuti, "Maye! wa m gwaz' o!" It occurs not unfrequently in songs.

Kepa nga vuka kusasa, nga ba tshela abantu, nga ti, "In*h*liziyo yami imbi. Nga pupa umjadu, nga pupa isililo." Ba ti abantu, "Into embi o i pupileyo. Umjadu isililo. Loku wa shiya ekaya ku gulwa, isililo si ipupo eli*h*le; lelo 'pupo lesililo a li nakcala; li*h*le, lo 'pupe isililo; ipupo elibi elomjadu. Ba ti futi, "Nalo lomjadu ngesinye isikati uma u ba u pupa, ize nje; ku ba nosuku nje, li ti lona elibi ipupo li k*q*amb' amanga nje."

And I woke in the morning and told the people, saying, "My heart is heavy. I have dreamt of a wedding-dance, and of a funeral lamentation." The people said, "You have dreamt of a bad thing. A wedding-dance is a sign that there will be a funeral lamentation. Since when you left home there was someone ill, the funeral lamentation is a good dream; the dream of a wedding is of no consequence; your dream of a funeral lamentation is good; the dream of a wedding is bad." They further said, "And sometimes if you frequently dream of a wedding, it is nothing; or if you dream of it once only, it is not a sign that can be depended on."

Nga ti mina, "Nga ka nga u pupa umjadu. Ani[94] a ku lungile ekaya. Anti[94] umkwekazi wami u bubile."

I said, "Some time ago I dreamt of a wedding. When I awoke I said, 'It is not right at home. My mother-in-law is dead.'"

Ngi be ngi s' and' ukupupa wona umjadu, kwa fika umuntu, nga tshaywa uvalo. Uma ngi sa m bona lo 'muntu, nga puma endhlini yokupeka, nga m bingelela, nga ti, "Sa ku bona." Nga ti, "Kona ngi ku bingelela nje, ngi ku bone k*q*ede, nga tshaywa uvalo; kwa nga ti i kona indaba o za 'ku ngi tshela." Ngoba ngi m bone k*q*ede, nga tshaywa uvalo. Wa ti, "O, kuloko, uvalo lokutshaya ngakona. Ekaya le ku kona in-

Immediately after I had dreamt of the wedding, a man came, and I was alarmed. As soon as I saw him I went out of the cooking house, and saluted him, and said, "Although I thus salute you, as soon as I saw you I felt alarmed; it felt as if there was something you have come to tell me." For as soon as I saw him I felt alarmed. He said, "O, you felt alarm with reason. There is bad news

[94] Dialectic for *kanti*.

daba embi. Umkwekazi wako u bubile." Nga ti mina, "U bube isifo si ni na?" Wa ti, "Wa bika empinjeni; wa ti, 'Kubu*h*lungu lapa.'" Wa ti, "Ka banga nalusuku; usuku s' ezwa se ku kalwa isililo nje. Sa dinga uma ku fe mupi umuntu. Sa buza tina ukuti, 'Ini na? Ku kalwa nje, kw enze njani na?' 'Ku bube umkwekazi kaguaise.' Sa buza ukuti, 'U be nani na? Loku na kutangi si be si naye na, e nga guli na?' 'Au, a s' azi, nati si y' etuka nje. Nati si zwa ngaso isililo nje.' 'Au, ku tiwa ukufa kuni na?' 'Au, wa bika empinjeni; wa ti, Kubu*h*lungu umpimbo; wa ti, Wa kwelwa in*h*loko; wa ba se u ya fa.'"

at your home. Your mother-in-law is dead." I said, "Of what disease did she die?" He said, "She complained of pain in her throat. And on that very day we heard the funeral lamentation. We could not tell who had died. But asked, 'What is it? Since there is lamentation, what has happened?' They said, 'Uguaise's mother-in-law is dead.' We asked, 'What was the disease? For only the day before yesterday we were with her, and she was not ill?' They answered, 'O, we do not know, and we too are startled. We too hear only by the lamentation.' We said, 'O, what disease is it said to be?' They said, 'She complained of pain in her windpipe. Then her head was affected, and she died.'"

Abantu ba mangala umuntu ukufa e nga gulanga. Kwa ba kona abantu, ba ti, "A ku yiwe ezinyangeni, ku yozwakala lesi 'sifo esi m bulala umuntu e nga gulanga."

Kwa yiwa ezinyangeni. Izinyanga za fika za ti, "U bulewe umuntu. Lowo 'muntu umkulu o m buleleyo; u nzanele ukukqeda lowo 'muzi; umuntu omkulu, umunumuzana."

Ngi ti ke, "Ngi pupe nam*h*la nje, nga tshaywa uvalo. In*h*liziyo

The man wondered at death when the person was not ill. And some said, "Let us go to the diviners, that we may hear what the disease is which kills a man without his having been ill."

They went to the diviners. The diviners said, "She has been killed by someone. He who has killed her is a great man; he wishes to destroy the village; he is a great man, a captain of villages."

So I say, "I have dreamt today, and am alarmed. My heart

ya kumbula lawo 'mapupo a ng' enza ngapambili; in*hl*iziyo yami ya ti, 'Umakazi leli 'pupo lomjadu li ngi *hl*onze nje, uma kulungile nje na ekaya na? Loku nga shiya ku gula umfazi wami, ku gul' umame. Ini ukuba ngi pupe ipupo e nga li pupa kuk*q*ala, kwa bonakala na?"

remembers the dreams which I formerly dreamt; and my heart asks, 'Can it be, since this dream of a wedding comes to me again, that it is not right at my home? For when I left my home, my wife and mother were ill. Why have I dreamt a dream which I dreamt formerly and it came true?'"

Ba pendula ba ti abakwiti Umpengula, ba ti, "O, libi ipupo lomjadu. In*hl*iziyo yako imbi ngakona; ipupo lomjadu li fana nepupo lokuba ku gula umuntu. Uma u m pupa e gula kakulu, u nga m pupa e kulupele, e fak' izinto zake zonke ezin*hl*e, impa*hl*a yake; lo 'muntu u ba u file; ka sindi. Umuntu um' e gula, ku ba ku*hl*e u m pupe e file, e kalelwa isililo; lo 'muntu ke u ya 'usinda; a ka yi 'kufa."

Our people, Umpengula and the rest, answered me, saying, "The dream of a wedding is a bad sign. Your heart is heavy with reason; to dream of a wedding is like dreaming that a man is ill. If you dream of him when he is very ill, you may dream that he is fat, and decked in his fine things; and that man is dead; he does not get well. When a man is ill, it is well to dream he is dead, and that they are weeping for him; then that man will get well; he will not die."

O tsho njalo kumina, ku pendula Umpengula; wa ti, "Ehe, guaise, kodwa i 'kuba u pupe umjadu, umjadu u 'pupo 'libi." A ti Uklas, "O, loko, guaise, elinye ipupo li se li ti lona; ipupo umuntu u li pupe ngesinye isikati, u pupe nje, ku nga veli 'luto."

It was Umpengula who answered me thus; and he said, "Yes, yes, Uguaise, but since you have dreamed of a wedding-dance, a wedding-dance is a bad dream." And Uklass answered, "O, as to that, Uguaise, one dream will turn out to be a bad omen; and a man may dream the same dream another time, and it turn out to be but a dream, and nothing come of it."

A ti Umpengula, "Ehe, u k*q*i-

Umpengula answered, "Yes,

nisile, klas, ku ba njalo ngesinye isikati; umuntu u pupa nje omunye, ku nga veli 'luto." Wa ti Umpengula, "Nami, guaise, nga ka nga li pupa nami ipupo. Ku gula Undayeni. E gula, nga pupa e vunule impa*hl*a yake, wa binca umuntsha wake wezinsimba, e fake amatshob' ake; nga pupa ku ketwa. Nga vuka kusasa nami, guaise, nga vuka in*hl*iziyo yami imbi. Nga ba lauzela abantu, nga ti ngi *hl*ezi nje, ngi bhekile, nga bona ku ti kcatsha izinyembezi eme*hl*weni ami. Nga ti mina, "Uma u file Undayeni—' Ngi te ngi sa ku gcina loko,—lo ngi sesilungwini, ngi ya sebenza,—ngi te, 'Ngi za 'ugukqula ame*hl*o emzileni,' nga m bona umfana; owakwiti lo 'mfana. Nga ti mina, 'O, u file Undayeni. Lo 'mfana u se zoku ngi bikela.' U te e sa fika, nga ti mina, 'Kona, mfana, u fika nje, ngi ti, u file Undayeni.' Wa ti umfana, 'Ehe, ngi fike nje, ngi zokubikela wena ukuti u file Undayeni.' Nga ti mina, 'Nami be se ngi bonile njalo ke.'"

yes, you say truly, Uklass, it is so sometimes; a man dreams merely of another, and nothing comes of it. And I too, Uguaise, once dreamt a dream. Undayeni was ill. During his illness I dreamt I saw him dressed in his best attire, with his umuntsha of wild cat's skins, and having put on his tails; I dreamt there was a dance. I awoke in the morning, Uguaise, with my heart depressed. I told the people my dream, and remained waiting, my eyes filling with tears. I said, 'If Undayeni is dead—' As I was saying those words,—for I was working with the white men,—I said, 'I will turn my eyes towards the road,' and I saw a lad coming; it was a lad belonging to us. I said, 'O, Undayeni is dead. The lad is coming to tell us.' As soon as he came I said to him, 'Lad, you have come because Undayeni is dead.' The boy said, 'Yes, yes; I come merely for the purpose of telling you that Undayeni is dead.' I replied, 'I too had already seen that it was so.'"

A i se vi mbi in*hl*iziyo yami. I ya kuluma kodwa, i ti, uma nga ku kona indaba, ngapana ngi bona ku fike umuntu o za 'ku ngi tshela. In*hl*iziyo yami i bona lona leli 'zwi eli tshiwo amadoda akwiti; nami se ngi ya bona ukuti, uma ku kona

My heart is no longer heavy. But it says if there is any thing the matter, I shall see someone coming to tell me. My heart sees that what the men of the place say is true; and I too now see that if

indaba, ngapana si fika isigijimi kumina ukuza 'u ngi bikela. Kodwa ngi sa bhekisisile, in*h*liziyo yami i ya 'udela k*q*ede ku k*q*ubeke izinsuku ngasemuva kwokupupa kwami. Ng' and' ukuba ngi ti, "Ai, a ku 'ndaba. Ubutongo kodwa bu ngi kwele ngamaongo-ongo."

UGUAISE.

there is any thing the matter I shall see a messenger coming to tell me. But I am still in deep expectation, and my heart will be satisfied when many days have passed after the dream. Then I shall say, "No, there is nothing the matter. But sleep has filled my mind with mere senseless images."

Subjective Apparitions.

KWA ti ngalezo 'nto ezi izilo ezi bonwa umuntu lapa e ti u ye 'kukuleka ngasese, nami nga ku bona loko futifuti. Lapa ngi ti ngi ya k*q*ala nje ukuguk*q*a, kumbe ilizwi lokuk*q*ala e ngi li tshoyo ngi ya li tsho, se ku kona okunye o se ku k*q*ala ukusondela; njengokuti, "Manje u wa valile ame*h*lo, ka sa yi 'ku ngi bona; a ngi sondele, ngi m lume, noma ngi m bambe, noma ngi m gwaze." Uma ngi ti ngi ya k*q*inisela, ng' ala ukuvuka, O, masinyane kwa fika umsindo omningi wokuk*q*eda isibindi, nokuba ku be kona ukuti, "Ku k*q*inisile. Okwokuk*q*ala ku be kuncinane; manje se ku fike okukulu oku za 'ku ngi bulala."

Lezo 'zinto zi njalonjalo ukufika kwazo, zi fika ngazinye; ku fike inyoka i name*h*lo amakulu, i nokwesabeka, ukuba lapo ngi guk*q*e

As regards those wild animals which a man sees when he is going to pray in secret, I too have seen them again and again. When I was beginning to kneel, or when I was saying the first word perhaps, there was something beginning to approach me; as though it said, "Now he has closed his eyes, and will no longer see me; let me draw near and bite him, or lay hold of him, or stab him." If I steadily refused to arise, O, at once there came a great noise which took away all my courage, and led me to say, "This is something real. The first was a little thing; now there is coming a great thing to kill me."

When these things come to any one they always come separately; there comes a snake with great eyes and very fearful; so that

kona, ngi nga be ngi sa k*q*inisela, ngi ya 'kuvuka.

Uma ku nge si yo, ku fika isilo si hamba ngokunyenya ukuze si ngi bambe, loku ngi nga boni, ngi bheke pansi, ngi ti ngi ya kuleka enkosini. Kepa ukukuleka kwami ku nga be ku sa k*q*ina; ngi k*q*ale ukukuleka kancinane ngapakati, ng' enza izikau, ukuze ind*h*lebe yami i nga bi ekukulekeni kodwa, i be na sekulaleleni ukuk*q*wabaza kwesilo si hamba ngoku ngi zuma. Uma se ngi bona ngokuba pela ku njalo, ku ti uma ngi bone ukuti, "O, manje sa k*q*ala ukulunga ukuze si ngi bambe," ngi vuke lapo.

Futi uma ku nge si so isilo, umuntu o ngi zondayo, u pete umkonto, umude, 'enzela ukuze a ngi gwaze, ngi fele kuleso 'sikund*h*la; naye u hamba ngokunyonyoba, ukuze ngi nga mu zwa.

Lokupela ku njalonjalo, ku ngokuba uma umuntu e ya ngapand*h*le u be e nga kuleki ngen*h*liziyo, kodwa u be kuluma a pumisele; kepa ke ku ngaloko lezo 'zilo e be zi ngi bona zi be zi ngi bona ngokuzwa ukuvungazela; kepa zi sondele. Nalowo 'muntu ngi ya m bona uma e se pakamisa ingalo ukuze a ngi gwaze; ngi ya bona noma e se e linga uku ngi gwaza impela.

when I have knelt, I could not remain firm, but rose up again.

If it was not a snake, a leopard would come on stealthily to lay hold of me, for I could not see, but was looking on the ground, intending to pray to the Lord. But my prayer was no longer steady; I began to pray a little in my heart, praying and stopping that my ear may not only listen to my prayer, but also to the crackling made by the leopard as it came to seize me. When I saw that it was something real, and that the leopard was preparing itself to seize me, I arose.

And if it was not a leopard, it would be a man who hated me, with a long assagai in his hand, approaching to kill me, that I may die in that place; and he too went stealthily, that I might not hear him.

For under these circumstances a man who went out to pray would not pray with the heart only, but speak aloud; therefore those animals saw me because they heard the murmuring of my voice; and drew near. And I saw the man when he raised his arm to stab me, or when he really tried to thrust the assagai into my body.

Lokupela ku njalonjalo ngi ya kuleka, a ngi sa kuleki nganhliziyo 'nye, se ngi kuleka ngamapuputu, ngi tanda ukuba ngi buke masinyane kuleyo 'ndawo, ngokuba ngi ya bulawa.

A ti uma lowo 'muntu e se ngi gwaza, ngi vuke, nalelo 'lizwi e be ngi kuluma ngalo li nga ka peli; se li pumile lona, kepa ngi nga ka li kqedi, li nqamuke kabili. Ngi vuke ukuze ngi sinde. Ukuvuka kwami ngi vuke ngokwetuka, ngi kqalaze ngalapo lowo 'muntu e vele ngakona, ngi nga m boni.

Ku nga be ku sa ba ko ukuba ngi buyele ekukulekeni, ngi kqedele loko e be ngi tanda uku ku tsho. Hai! Se ku pelile; a ngi sa ku boni ngaleso 'sibelu esi ngi tusileyo. O, kwa za kw' anela. Ku i loko njalo ekukulekeni. Ngi ya vuka se ngi jambile, ngokuba ng' etuswe amanga, nga kolwa. Kepa nga za nga ku bona loko, ukuti, ku amanga, nokuba kw' enziwa ngokuba ngi be ngi puma ku se luvivi, ngi ba shiye be sa lele, ng' enzela ukuti, kona ngi ya 'kuba nesikati sokuzikulekela enkosini; ngokuba uma ngi puma se ku sile, nabo se be pumile ukuya 'kwenza imisebenzana yabo, noma ukuya ngapandhle; ba be se be

When I prayed under such circumstances I no longer prayed with singleness of heart, but in a hurry, wishing to look without delay to the place from which the danger threatened me, for I was in danger.

And when the man was now stabbing me, I would arise, the sentence which I was uttering being unfinished; it was already begun but not ended, but cut in two. I arose that I might escape. When I arose I arose with a start, and looked to the place whence the man came; but did not see him.

It was no longer possible for me to return to my prayers and finish what I had begun to say. No! There was now an end of it, and I could no longer say what I wanted for the false alarm which had frightened me. O, this was repeated again and again. It happened continually in my prayers. I arose ashamed because I had been frightened by fantacy, and believed in it. But at length I saw that it was fantacy, and that it happened because I went out before it was light, leaving the people still asleep, doing so because I should then have time to pray for myself to the Lord; for if I went out while it was day, they too would have gone out to do their daily work, and would hear,

ngi zwa, ba *h*lebelane ngami ukuti, "O, lo 'muntu u se u ya kolwa; ngi m zwile e kuleka; ku*h*le ukuba a ti lapo e kuleka kona, si hambe, si ye 'ku m vusa, noma si m tshaye, ukuze a nga be e sa pinda lezo 'zinto."

Ezi izilo nga zi bona ngokupuma ku se mnyama, ku nga ka kanyi ukusa. Kepa ukuze ngi bone ukuti a ku 'siminya nga bona ngokuba ku ze amasuku a ze 'anele ku njalonjalo, nga ze nga zi dela, ukuti, "Au, ku ya 'kusiza ini ukuba ngi ti lapa ngi kuleka ngi vuswe izilwanyana ezi ngi d*h*layo, kanti a zi ko? loku ngi nga zuzi nje loko e ngi ku vukela enkosini, ngi vinjelwa izilo e ngi zi bonayo. Ake ngi k*q*inisele ngi ze ngi zwe se zi ngi bamba impela, ngi pikelele ukukuleka njalo."

Nembala nga ti ngi sa guk*q*a, sa fika isilwanyana esi inyoka ukwenza okwemisuku. Nga ti, "Ai! Nam*h*la a ngi zwe ngomzimba ukuti se si ngi bambile." Ng' a*h*lula lapo. Kwa fika isilo esikulu. Nga ti na kuso, "A ngi zwe ngomzimba." Ng' a*h*lula. Kwa fika umuntu 'eza e gijima ukuze a ngi n*q*ume masinyane. Loku ngi s' eisile isilo, naye nga ti, "Ngi ya

and whisper about me one to another, saying, "O, that man is now a believer; I heard him praying; it is well for us to go to the place where he prays, and arouse him, or beat him, that he may not repeat such things."

The animals I saw because I went out whilst it was still dark, before the day had fully dawned. But at last I saw that it was not real because they appeared continually for many days, until I despised them, saying, "O, of what use will it be if when I pray I am made to arise from my knees by beasts which devour me, when forsooth they are not real? for I cannot get that for which I awake early to pray to the Lord, being prevented by the beasts which I see. Just let me strengthen myself until I feel them really seizing me, and persevere in prayer without ceasing."

And indeed when I was kneeling there came a snake to do as on other days. I said, "No! To-day let me feel by my body that it has already seized me." Then I conquered. There came a huge leopard. I said also to it, "Let me feel by my body." I conquered. There came a man, running to stab me at once. Since I had despised the leopard, I said too of the man, "Let me feel by my

'kuzwa ngomzimba." Nga m a*h*lula. Nga goduka ngi k*q*alabile, ukuti, "O, kanti ngi vinjelwe amanga."

Nga ti ngi pinda ukwenza njalo, a kwa be ku sa vama uku ng' esabisa. Kwa ya kwa pela, kwa ya kwa ti nya, ku ze ku be nam*h*la nje, a ku se ko. Abaningi ba vinjelwa i loko; lapo be ti ba ya k*q*ala nje ukukuleka, ba bone lezo 'zilwane ezi za 'ku ba d*h*la, ba vuke masinyane, ba goduke, a nga be e sa tsho umuntu ukuti, "Ngi ya 'kupinda ngi ye kuleyo 'ndawo;" a se ti, "Ngomso ku*h*le ngi ye ngalapa, ngi bone uma ku ya 'kuba njalo na." Ku be njalo; a *h*lale e se saba omunye. Ku njalo kwabanye. Kepa kwabaningi ku amanga njalo; ngokuba omunye uma e se vinjelwe, u ze a zibike ngokuti, "Au, ngi ya mangala kambe, ngokuba ngi ya k*q*utshwa ukuba ngi kuleke enkosini. Kepa ngi nga ka ti leke nokuti leke nje, O, nasi isilwane, nenyoka, nomuntu; loku ku fikela uku ngi bulala, se ngi vuka, ngi vinjelwe i lezo 'zinto." A miswe isibindi u lowo okwa ka kw' enza njalo kuye; a ti, "A ku 'luto loko; noma u bona into enjalo, u nga buki; ku*h*le

body." I conquered him. I went home having ascended a rock of safety, saying, "O, forsooth I have been hindered by fantasies."

I did so again, and the things no longer continued to frighten me. And at last they ceased altogether, and have not returned to the present day. Many are hindered by such things; when they merely begin to pray, they see these beasts which come to devour them, and they at once start and go up, and no one thinks of going to the same place again; but a man says, "To-morrow it will be well for me to go to such a place, and see if the same thing will happen again." It does happen again; and he is afraid ever after. Thus it happens with some. But with the generality these things are known to be fantasies; for if a man is hindered by them, he tells some one else, saying, "O, I wonder, for I am impelled to pray to the Lord. But before I begin to open my mouth, lo, there is a beast, a snake, or a man; these come to kill me, and I start up and am hindered by these things." He is encouraged by the other to whom the same thing has happened; he says, "It is nothing; though you do see such things, do not look; it is proper

ukuba u k*q*inisele; u ya 'ugoduka; a ku yi 'kud*h*liwa impela njengokungati u za 'kud*h*liwa." Nembala ku be njalo; a buye e se e ncoma ukuti, "O, kanti ngi ko*h*liswa amanga, 'bani."

UMPENGULA MBANDA.

to be firm; you will go home uninjured; you will not be really devoured as it appears to you that you will be." And so it turns out; and he tells his friend, "O, So-and-so, forsooth I was deceived by fantasies."

KWA ti ngesikati sokulungiselwa kwami ukubapatiswa, nga ngi zinge ngi tandaza njalo ngezikati zonke ngasese. Ng' enza njalo ngoba ku ti lapo ngi tandazayo ku be njengokuba ya ngi bona impela inkosi. Ngi y' esuka lapo, in*h*liziyo yami i kcakcambile kakulu. Ng' enza njalo ngoba ngi bona ukuti, "Ku nga ba ku*h*le ukuba ngi kolwe kuyo inkosi, ngi be umntwana wayo nami." Kepa ku ti ngesinye isikati la ngi tandazayo ngi bone ku fika isilwane esibi, ku nga ti si ya 'ku ngi limaza. Ng' etuke, ngi shiye ukutandaza; kanti ka ngi boni 'luto. Kwa ba njalo ngezikati ezibili. Kwa ti ngesobutatu nga k*q*inisela, nga ti, "Ake ngi bone uma si za 'ku ngi limaza ini na?" Nga k*q*inisela, nga za nga k*q*eda ukutandaza. Ka nga be ngi sa bona 'luto uma se ngi k*q*edile. Nga balisa ngaloko, nga ti, "Ku ini loku?" Kepa nga se ngi zwile ngapambili ngamakolwa ukuti, "Uma umuntu e tandaza yedwa, u ya fikelwa izinto ezimbi

IT happened when I was being instructed for baptism, I used habitually to pray at all times in secret. I did so because when I prayed it was as if I really saw the Lord; and I went away from prayer with my heart very white indeed. I did so because I saw that it would be well for me too to believe in the Lord, and to become His child. But once when I was praying I saw a venomous beast coming to me as though it was about to injure me. I started up and left off praying. But forsooth I saw nothing. This happened twice; but on the third time I strengthened myself and said, "Let me just see if it will injure me or no." I strengthened myself till I had ended my prayer. And I saw nothing when I had finished. I doubted about it, and asked what it meant. But I had already heard from believers that when a man prayed alone, venomous creatures came to him when

uma zi kqutshwa Usatan." Nga bona ngaloko ukuti, "Ngi lingwa Usatan nje." Kepa ku zinge kw enza njalo njalo ngezikati zonke. Kwa za kwa ti ngemva kwesibindi sami, nga bona ukuti, "Ku ize nje." Kwa fika ngamandhla ukukanya okukulu; nga buya nga ti, uma ngi bona ukukanya okugcweleyo kumina, ngi buye ngi zisole ngi ti, "Ku ini ukuba ngi zinge ng' etuka into e ize nje na?" Kepa nga kqinisa ngamandhla enkosi, ngi bona ukuti, "Inkosi i nami ngezikati zonke." Emva kwaloko uma ngi tandaza ngi bona ukuti, "Inkosi i kona; ku nga ti ngi ng' andiza ngi ye kona ngokujabula okukcikcimayo enhliziyweni yami." Kwa ba njalo ke. Kepa a ngi tsho ukuti ngi wa kqeda onke amagama amanye e nga ngi wa bona ngaleso 'sikati, kwa za kwa fika isikati sokubapatizwa kwami.

USETEMBA DHLADHLA.

they were urged on by Satan. I saw by that that I was merely tempted by Satan. But this continued without cessation, until I took courage, and saw that it was nothing. And then there came with power a great light to me; and when I found myself full of light, I reproved myself for being continually startled by nothing. But I strengthened myself with the strength of the Lord, and saw that He was with me always. After that when I prayed I saw that the Lord is, and it was as if I could fly away to Him for the joy which overflowed my heart. So it was. But I do not say that I have mentioned every thing that I saw at that time before the time came for me to be baptised.[95]

---

95 The reader will see repeated in these narratives the experiences of St. Antony, Hilarion, and other early saints.

INKOSAZANA.[96]

The following superstition as regards the Inkosazana appears to be the relic of some old worship; and is therefore properly considered in this place.

Indaba ngenkosazana eya vela m*h*la ku vela abantu em*h*labeni.

The account of the Inkosazana who came out on the same day that men came out of the earth.

A i vami ukubonwa ngame*h*lo. Si zwa ku tiwa y' aziwa abendulo. A ku ko namunye kwaba se kona owa ke wa i bona. Ku tiwa inyamazanyana encane, i ngangek*q*ak*q*a, i nemitshwana em*h*lotshana nemnyama; ngolunye u*h*langoti ku mile um*h*langa nama*h*lati notshani; ngolunye umuntu. I mile kanjalo ke.

She is not commonly seen. We hear it said the primitive men knew her. No one existing at the present time ever saw her. She is said to be a very little animal, as large as a polecat, and is marked with little white and black stripes; on one side there grows a bed of reeds, a forest, and grass;[97] the other side is that of a man. Such is her form.

Ku ti uma i *h*langana nomuntu i zifi*h*le, i kulume naye e nga i boni, 'ezwe izwi nje lokuti, "Fulatela; u nga ngi bheki, ngokuba ngi hamba-ze." I tsho ngokuba ngemuva isin*q*e sayo si bomvu beje. Nembala ke umuntu a nga be e sa bheka, a kolwe ukuba "I

If she meet with a man she conceals herself and speaks with him without his seeing her; he hears only a voice saying to him, "Turn your back; do not look on me, for I am naked." Saying thus because her buttocks are red like fire. And so the man no longer looks in that direction, but believes that

[96] *Inkosazana*, Princess, or Little Chieftainess.

[97] Not, says the native who gives the narrative, to be understood literally; but that there was something growing on her like a bed of reeds, a forest, and grass. But compare Ugungg*q*u-kubantwana, *Zulu Nursery Tales*, p. 176; and Usilosimapundu, p. 184.

yo inkosazana e ngi za ngi zwa indaba yayo. I yo ke le." A fulatele ngokwesaba ukuba ku tiwa uma umuntu e i bonile, wa bhekana nayo, ka lungi, u ya fa masinyane.

I hamba nobu lwabantwana abaningi aba landela ngemuva, aba fana nayo.

Ku ti ngesinye isikati uma umuntu e i funyene ensimini i ti kuye, "Nonyaka u za 'kutola ukud*h*la; nakuba u kade u nend*h*lala, a u sa yi 'kuba nayo manje."

Futi i yona e veza imikuba eminingi pakati kwabantu abamnyama. I ti abantwana a ba kitshwe emabeleni, ba nga nceli; noma be bancane kakulu ba kitshwe masinyane ngezwi layo, ngokwesaba ukuti uma be nga kitshwa ku ya 'kuvela umkuba omubi kubantwana wokuba ba fe.

Y enza imiteto enjalo ke; imiteto yayo y enziwe, a i delelwa; ngokuba ku tiwa, "Ku tsho inkosazana." Nenkosi e busayo a i tsho ukuti insumansumane; izwi lenkosazana li ngapezulu kwelenkosi.

Lelo 'zwi lokuti a ku kitshwe abantwana, a i kulumi kubantu abaningi; i kuluma kumuntu e

it is indeed the Inkosazana about whom he has heard; and turns his back from fear, because it is said that if a man look on her face to face, he will be ill and very soon die.[98]

She goes followed by a large troop of children which resemble her.

Sometimes if a man meet with her in his garden she says to him, "This year you shall have food; although for a long time there has been famine, it shall be so no longer."

Besides it is she who introduces many fashions among black men. She orders the children to be weaned; and although they are very young, they are at once weaned in obedience to her commands, for they are afraid if they do not wean them they will be seized with some disease and die.

She makes such laws as these; and her laws are obeyed and not despised; for they say, "The Inkosazana has said." And the reigning chief does not say it is a fable; the word of the Inkosazana is greater than the chief's.

When she orders the children to be weaned she does not speak to many people; she speaks but to

[98] It may be interesting to compare this superstition with the following passages:—Exodus xxxiii. 20; Genesis xxxii. 30; Judges vi. 22, xiii. 22, 23.

www.ingramcontent.com/pod-product-compliance
Ingram Content Group UK Ltd.
Pitfield, Milton Keynes, MK11 3LW, UK
UKHW021306131025
8355UKWH00045B/1511